Praise for *Revolution in*
and Tom Szaky

"There are lots of great companies commi[...] we need many more. Tom Szaky's TerraCycle is doing more than selling good green products; it is changing how manufacturers, retailers, and consumers treat their waste. His persistence and courage in overcoming a huge challenge from Miracle-Gro reminded me of Ben & Jerry's similar struggle with Häagen-Dazs. Read this book. I'm glad I did."

—Ben Cohen, founder, Ben & Jerry's Ice Cream

"Warning, reading this book will cause you to quit everything to become an eco-entrepreneur! If you want to feel hopeful about our planet, and our ability to solve the ecological mess we've created, then stop everything and read this inspiring book. Tom Szaky represents the kind of optimistic yet pragmatic ingenuity that can turn this ship around. His quest to turn waste into profits is not only clever and rewarding, but his positive, can-do spirit is delightfully contagious."

—Gary Hirshberg, president and CE-Yo, Stonyfield Farm

"Like TerraCycle, The Body Shop started in a small corner of a little town with a big idea that defined our mission and fueled the company's path to success and growth. Tom Szaky's big idea, capitalizing on wasted waste, is not only a formula for good business, it is also favorably changing the way individuals, manufacturers, and retailers participate in the unfortunate chain of nonrecyclable packaging."

—Gordon Roddick, cofounder and former CEO,
The Body Shop International

"Ecopreneurs are still a rare species today. *Revolution in a Bottle* will motivate and educate any reader on how to become one. Ecopreneurs, like Tom Szaky, will revolutionize and save the economy and planet's future through their leadership. It is desperately needed for planetary restoration." —Horst Rechelbacher, founder, Aveda

"In a time when we are facing both an economic and ecological crisis, this book is a breath of fresh air. Tom Szaky is smart and inspiring, and his work is redefining how to do business in the climate era."

—Tzeporah Berman, cofounder,
ForestEthics and PowerUp Canada

Media quotes for *Revolution in a Bottle*:

"Szaky has written the best book on entrepreneurship I've read. This is not the story of a huge exit, or wow technology, or big money from top-tier VCs. It's the witty, funny, poignant tale of a young Princeton drop-out who finds himself up to his elbows in worm poop turned fertilizer on the way to building a pioneering 'upcycling' company, TerraCycle."
—Daniel Isenberg, *Harvard Business Review*

"Steve Jobs or Michael Dell he isn't (yet), but *Revolution in a Bottle* is a fun read that captures the restless, extemporizing life of the start-up entrepreneur." —David Price, *The Wall Street Journal*

"I do not usually want to read extracts from business books to my wife. But how many start-ups are troubled by neighbourhood gun fire between rival urban gangs, or become indirect beneficiaries of a scheme involving the farmers of America that was built around vermicompost, or worm excrement?" —Jonathan Birchall, *Financial Times*

"TerraCycle is an innovative, determined company that turned a seemingly kooky idea into an Earth-friendly moneymaker."
—Linda M. Castellitto, *USA Today*

"More than musings on the value of rubbish, this book offers an inspirational tale and sound advice for aspiring eco-entrepreneurs."
—*Sierra*

"This lively, anecdotal account is also a thoughtful examination of Szaky's cost-effective, environmentally friendly methods, demonstrating how 'turn[ing] a vicious cycle into a virtuous one' is not just possible, but profitable." —*Publishers Weekly*

"This is a five-star book that every environmentalist should read even if they don't think they're an entrepreneur and every entrepreneur should read even if they don't care about green." —GreenBiz.com

"Tom Szaky's news is a must-read for green entrepreneurs. Far from the usual boring business book, *Revolution in a Bottle* is a fast-paced entertaining read, chronicling TerraCycle's many near-catastrophes as well as with Tom's own thoughts on waste, eco-capitalism, green consumer habits, and PR strategies." —*Mother Nature Network*

PORTFOLIO/PENGUIN

REVOLUTION IN A BOTTLE

TOM SZAKY is the founder and CEO of TeraCycle, a global company that makes non-recyclable waste from chip bags to dirty diapers nationally recyclable. He also blogs for *The New York Times*, *Treehugger*, *The Huffington Post*, *Packaging Digest*, and many other publications, as well as stars in the National Geographic television show *Garbage Moguls*.

REVOLUTION

IN A BOTTLE

How to Eliminate the Idea of Waste

TOM SZAKY

PORTFOLIO/PENGUIN

PORTFOLIO/PENGUIN
Published by the Penguin Group
Penguin Group (USA) Inc., 375 Hudson Street, New York, New York 10014, USA
Penguin Group (Canada), 90 Eglinton Avenue East, Suite 700, Toronto, Ontario
M4P 2Y3, Canada (a division of Pearson Penguin Canada Inc.)
Penguin Books Ltd, 80 Strand, London WC2R 0RL, England
Penguin Ireland, 25 St Stephen's Green, Dublin 2, Ireland
(a division of Penguin Books Ltd)
Penguin Group (Australia), 707 Collins Street, Melbourne, Victoria 3008, Australia
(a division of Pearson Australia Group Pty Ltd)
Penguin Books India Pvt Ltd, 11 Community Centre, Panchsheel Park,
New Delhi – 110 017, India
Penguin Group (NZ), 67 Apollo Drive, Rosedale, Auckland 0632,
New Zealand (a division of Pearson New Zealand Ltd)
Penguin Books (South Africa), Rosebank Office Park, 181 Jan Smuts Avenue,
Parktown North 2193, South Africa
Penguin China, B7 Jiaming Center, 27 East Third Ring Road North,
Chaoyang District, Beijing 100020, China

Penguin Books Ltd, Registered Offices:
80 Strand, London WC2R 0RL, England

First published in the United States of America by Portfolio, a member of
Penguin Group (USA) Inc. 2009
This revised paperback edition published 2013

1   3   5   7   9   10   8   6   4   2

LIBRARY OF CONGRESS CATALOGING-IN-PUBLICATION DATA
Szaky, Tom.
Revolution in a bottle: how to eliminate the idea of waste / Tom Szaky.—
Revised paperback edition.
pages cm
ISBN 978-1-59184-250-7
ISBN 978-1-59184-595-9
1. TerraCycle Plant Food (Firm)   2. Fertilizer industry—United States.
3. Waste products as fertilizer—United States.   4. Organic fertilizers—
United States.   5. Green products—United States.   I. Title.
HD9483.U54T47 2013
338.7'631870973—dc23   2012040617

Printed in the United States of America

Contents

Foreword

Don't read *Revolution in a Bottle* **like** literature or a case study. This is not a ripe "I-did-it-my-way" vanity by someone who lucked out and made a lot of money. This is an overture to the shadow of modernity, a pulsing story of incipient commerce that is the birth of a new asset class: the unrecyclable industry. Tom Szaky invented a new category of business, a company functioning like a detritivore that fractions industrial waste into ingenious new products that feed retail environments. Szaky is an entrepreneurial Princeton dropout who never saw a waste problem he couldn't remedy. The problem he solves is the incalculable volume of garbage generated by factories because of the badly designed take-make-waste system of industrial civilization. His paradigm is simple: unwanted molecules of industry equal feedstock for TerraCycle.

There are several things to do with waste. Throw it away and hope nature takes care of it. Incinerate it so that the molecules go someplace else, and hope nature takes care of it. Recycle it and when it is ultimately thrown away, hope nature takes care of it. Tom's method: pay me to take away the waste and let our people redesign it into something your customers will buy. Szaky's first product set the gold standard for waste: the shipping carton is garbage, the bottles are soda pop throwaways, the content is worm poop made from kitchen waste, and maybe, just maybe, this is the first time a Pepsi bottle contained something of value. In the trade, TerraCycle's worm poop in a bottle is known as upcycling. Take a material and make it more valuable than its first incarnation.

In the TerraCycle warehouse, Mylar overprints for shade-grown coffee bags cover Starbucks journals. Kool-Aid packets become pencil holders for Target. TerraCycle makes Oreo messenger bags, Capri Sun tote bags, Clif Bar backpacks, and newspaper pencils galore. You don't merely have a corporate logo on your knapsack, you are a walking cookie package. Szaky's products would have destroyed Andy Warhol's career in a prior decade. The number of SKUs climbs with every season. Szaky's business is like a delectable group of edible toadstools growing out of the muck.

Foreword

This mash-up of consumerism and material cycling has extensive commercial implications. Conceivably, TerraCycle could be the first company that has negative cost of goods. Competitors have already taken notice. TerraCycle is taking materials from the shadow side of industrial practices and bringing them back to light as products other companies want to pay to have made. The long-term implications are even more mind-boggling. What if most industrial waste streams are banned from landfills and incinerators, as is becoming the case in Europe and Japan? Who are you going to call? In other words, rather than acting as an outlet for overruns and abandoned SKUs, TerraCycle could become an integral part of product planning for many, many companies, in addition to the several Fortune 500 companies it already serves. What happens then is a symbiotic relationship, which is exactly the type of relationship that a detritivore has with its environment. An insect munches the dead and decomposing waste from a tree, and its waste in turn enriches the soil that feeds the tree, which feeds the detritivore, and we call that relationship life, an extensive integration of mutualism where all parties benefit.

The impression you get from Szaky is an unabashed, bring-it-on, joyful celebration of the discarded, marginal, and hidden. When you see the lineup of iconic corporate logos emblazoning TerraCycle's product line, you know there is not a trace of doubt in Szaky. He looks disbelievingly at those who question his all-out effort to place his goods in Walmart,

Target, and Home Depot. He is proud of his wares, knowing that they are inexpensive and available to every American pocketbook. Every item TerraCycle uses would otherwise be burned or buried by now. Instead of occupying a landfill, his TerraCycle pencil holders contain TerraCycle pencils in Terra-Cycle knapsacks protected by TerraCycle umbrellas held by children whose clothes were washed in green TerraCycle cleaners packaged in sixty-four-ounce soda bottles.

Waste has negative value in economic terms. In nature, waste is manna, and it is becoming gold in the world of Tom Szaky. Alchemy is the story here. It is the magic of passion, brilliance, and persistence coupled with the belief that we are our litter's keeper. For every hopeful green entrepreneur reading this book, note that Szaky's original business knowledge couldn't fill a thimble. But his business imagination filled the earth. This is rare. His vision benefits the earth, the poor, and the giant corporations at the same time. Such an idea attracts all the business knowledge it needs and creates its own universe of intelligence. Eventually it becomes the new conventional wisdom and students will study it in schools, but by then there will be new Tom Szakys outraging the norms. In a world where our collective prospects seem bleak if not absent, the best thing we can do is create a livable future, proving that there is no such thing as inconsequential action. Tom Szaky is focused on every discarded wrapper, bottle, mill end, and overrun. The grandness of this vision is grounded in minutiae. All the 10 septillion detritivores that keep our soils and waters fertile, nourished, and clean are cheering on Szaky. And so should we.

—PAUL HAWKEN

Coauthor of *Natural Capitalism*

and author of *Blessed Unrest*

Introduction

What is garbage?

It doesn't exist in nature, as every output (from a leaf falling off a tree to an animal taking a poop in the forest) is an important input for the system that eats it. We inhale the oxygen that a tree exhales; the carbon dioxide we exhale is inhaled by the tree.

Garbage does exist in the human system, however. It is modern—a more modern concept than we assume. If you think back to your parents' time, or perhaps their parents', garbage didn't exist the way it does today.

People used to value durableness, passing down plateware and kitchen tables to future generations. When something broke or tore, it was repaired; people made their livings cobbling worn-out shoes and mending torn shirts. And, when these things were ultimately disposed of, that which was made from natural materials (basically everything) ranging from wood to cotton would be easily absorbed by nature.

So what happened? After the Great Depression we entered into the biggest global war the world has ever experienced. Emerging from such despair required an economic mechanism to rebuild our economies and increase our standard of living. The idea of disposable products emerged, made possible by many newly invented and mass-producible complex synthetic materials (principally plastics). The challenge of these "miracle materials" is that nature doesn't know what to do with a plastic fork like it does a cotton shirt. As intended, the encouragement of consumption brought the economy around, and as our national GDPs grew, so, too, did the amount of waste produced per person.

The simplest answer to this conundrum is to stop buying stuff.

Corporations are simply responding to our desires. They are in the business of figuring out what we want and getting it to us so we buy it. If we buy a bag of chips or a pack of cigarettes, we are voting to make more chips and smokes. This daily vote is perhaps more important than the one we make every four years for the leader of our country. So be conscious of what you vote for with your dollars.

Introduction

Most of us are addicted to consumption, as am I. And it's hard for most of us right now to conceive of our lives without buying new products on a daily basis. So within that context, perhaps buy a glass container instead of a disposable one. Or buy a nice lighter that could last for years instead of a disposable one. What about a handkerchief instead of tissues?

In time, if followed by a majority of people, steps like these can make a difference, but in isolation, they are symbolic compared to the 5 billion tons of garbage we generate on a yearly basis.

While some waste streams are recyclable, the vast majority of our waste is nonrecyclable, which means that it cannot be recycled through traditional recycling systems. Therefore it ends up in either landfills or incinerators. These are the only two solutions to nonrecyclable waste today, and they treat waste like a problem instead of something of value. While most nonrecyclable waste can in fact be recycled (in other words, it's technically possible) the cost of collection and recycling is in all cases greater than the value of the material that is recovered. In other words, recyclability is not predicated on the availability of technical solutions (as they exist for basically everything), but on simple economics.

When waste is sent to a landfill (like the majority of nonrecyclable waste in the world) it simply sits there, creating leachate and methane and other nasty by-products, and perhaps one day, the landfill site gets covered over and made into a park.

Introduction

If the waste goes to an incineration facility (like the majority of waste in Germany and many other countries in western Europe) it is burned for the caloric (energy) value of the material, releasing tremendous amounts of carbon and other emissions into the air as well as leaving potentially toxic ash behind. And, ironically, 90 percent of global incineration facilities don't even attempt to produce energy from the waste that is burned.

Both of these solutions are noncyclical and effectively discard the massive amount of invested energy that was spent in extracting and refining raw materials from the earth to make the products. For example, the shirt you are wearing likely started as soil that grew into cotton, which was refined into a textile that was then sewn into your shirt. The metal in your cell phone started in a mine and the plastic originated from petroleum, which started as prehistoric plants, which in turn started as soil. If we spend so much energy and money extracting materials from the earth and refining them into amazing products, why do we discard them often after a single use?

The answer is economics. Consumption is the key driver for modern economic growth, and what better way to consume more and more, year after year, than having disposable products that force you to do so?

The answer to what is recyclable and what is not is also driven entirely by economics. The cost to collect and melt an aluminum can into ore is less than the ore's value on the market. The same economic issues hold true for rigid PET,

HDPE, simple paper, and glass. This is why they are globally recyclable materials. For everything else, it's cheaper to produce new virgin materials than to collect, sort, and recycle them. For example, collecting and recycling a candy wrapper or juice pouch is more expensive than the resulting plastic is worth. As there is no "market" at a price that justifies recycling, the waste stream is deemed "nonrecyclable."

In 2002 I dropped out of Princeton University to found TerraCycle, a company whose purpose is to eliminate the idea of waste. We make nonrecyclable waste recyclable by creating national collection and solution programs, often funded by the brands that make the products and packaging. Consumers send us (postage paid) their waste from anywhere in a given country. The collected waste is either reused (refurbishing clothing and electronics), upcycled (turning things like juice pouches into backpacks), or recycled (melting chip bags into plastic trash cans). As of mid-2012, TerraCycle was operating in twenty-two countries, with more than 30 million people sending millions of pieces of nonrecyclable waste every day.

It all started a decade earlier, by turning organic waste into worm poop, liquefying it, then packaging the stuff directly in used soda bottles, creating TerraCycle Plant Food.

Introduction

It's been a wild ride and I hope that in the chapters ahead you enjoy the front-row seat. I know that not every lesson I've learned or insight I've applied is universal; however, I trust that my experiences will be useful to those who wonder if they are ready to birth a new venture. Hold onto what you believe in, because your conviction can be infectious, and sometimes it's all that separates us from giving up.

—TOM SZAKY

Trenton, New Jersey

2012

CHAPTER 1

Up to My Neck

September 10, 2001, I landed in—of all places—New Jersey. I know what you're thinking, and once I landed so was I. I never knew where Princeton University was and was happy enough to get in, so I never bothered finding out until I looked at my plane ticket. To my surprise it read EWR ("Newark") . . . to be honest I thought it was a typo for "New York"—silly foreigner.

New Jersey is a gigantic suburb in between New York City and Philadelphia. It officially calls itself "the Garden State" and unofficially "the garbage state." If you've ever watched an episode of *The Sopranos* you'll know just how famous Jersey is for its own unique breed of waste management.

1

Revolution in a Bottle

By the end of freshman year you'd expect that I would have been pumped to leave New Jersey and go back to Canada for the summer as a camp counselor in the wilderness or take a fancy internship in New York City. Instead I decided to stay and start a worm poop company. For almost the whole of my freshman year I had been fascinated with the commercial potential of fairly ordinary earthworms (not the fishing kind)— red wigglers, *Eisenia fetida*—which thrive on food waste. They are voracious consumers of organic waste of all kinds, and their principal by-product, just like all animals' (including us), is poop ("worm castings,". in the language of the trade). Yet their poop, unlike ours, makes a terrific fertilizer.

The idea seemed to have some stellar economics behind it. People would pay me to take away their garbage, I figured; the worms would eat it—converting it into mountains of poop—and I would box up the poop and sell it. Seemed to me that the cost of my raw materials (the garbage) would be negative (since people would pay me to take it away), and what the worms pooped out people would also pay for. I could make money on both ends.

So during freshman year my friend Jon Beyer and I (with the help of a few innocent bystanders I was able to rope in with free Milwaukee's Best and PBR) had drafted a worm poop business plan, scraped together the cost of a machine that could house millions of worms and collect their poop, and convinced the university to give us the waste from one of its dining halls.

There I was, the first day of that hot, swampy summer in New Jersey, staring at a mountain of rotting, maggot-filled, yet quite colorful organic waste from one of Princeton's dining halls. Everything from half-eaten hot dogs to those less-than-popular Brussels sprouts were there. All mine!

Unfortunately, Jon had returned to Maryland to work as a waiter over the summer, reducing the staff of TerraCycle by 50 percent. Luckily I had convinced a senior named Noemi Millman to join us. She was a friend from the campus theater group and serendipitously someone who didn't have any firm plans for that summer. I convinced her to join TerraCycle without really telling her what the job entailed.

We were waiting for Harry. Harry Windle was the inventor and builder of the "worm gin," a fantastical machine that supposedly would transform mountains of organic waste into worm poop in record time (seven days, to be precise). A few months prior I had bought one of his machines, and Harry was on his way from Gainesville, Florida, to deliver it. He was even "giving" it to us for half price: $20,000. The university had agreed to let us use a small area nearby as a work site, a little patch of beaten-down grass and dirt perfect for our modest needs—and most importantly out of the way, as a prevailing easterly breeze would have doused the campus in a blanket of foul odor rivaling an unplugged fridge filled with months-old milk. In preparation for the arrival of the worm gin, Noemi and I had brought the crucial tools of our trade as worm poop farmers: a 1985 Rent-A-Wreck Ford pickup—rusty black—some shovels, and a wood chipper.

We needed the wood chipper because worms will eat just about anything that's organic and fresh, but they have small mouths that can't swallow anything that hasn't been deconstructed effectively into a porridgelike homogeneous sludge. The plan was to drive to the dining hall, load the buckets into our truck, and drive them out to the site. Once there, we'd open them up and start shoveling their contents into the wood chipper. Then we'd simply transfer the resulting sludge, of chopped maggots and rotting food, onto the worm gin's conveyor belt, where it would enter the machine and feed our worms.

All we needed now was Harry Windle and his worm gin. Harry was late. And Princeton had been collecting food waste for us from the dining hall for more than a week, so that we'd really be able to hit the ground running. I didn't lose confidence, though: he'd already built the gin—and I still owed him $10,000 for it. He would come.

Finally, two days after we were supposed to meet Harry, a massive red F-350 pickup truck crashed onto Washington

Road, bearing our unassembled worm gin. After it screeched to a stop in front of us, Harry climbed out, carrying his gallon jug of Dunkin' Donuts coffee, and said, "Wheah d'ya wannit?"

Harry was a tall, fifty-year-old man from the swamps of Gainesville. A man who had done everything from raising hundreds of bulldogs to buying a cow (Betsy), so he didn't have to mow his own grass, to inventing automatic worm poop machines. Harry stayed with us for a week to help set up the worm gin and get it going (and to get his money—which I purposely held out until everything was working). When it was assembled, the worm gin was a thing of beauty: imagine a Christmas tree built with very wide conveyer belts, six on each side of the "trunk," standing about fifteen feet high and twenty feet wide. The worms lived on the angled belts, partaking of the snowfall of garbage that would fall from a central hopper that sat on top.

Each conveyor belt moved away from the center very, very slowly—about an inch every five hours. The idea was that the worms would move up toward the food (away from their poop, since we know all animals, including us, don't like hanging out in their own poop) while the conveyor belt was moving down and away from the center—carrying the worm poop along. When the worm poop reached the bottom of the belt, it would simply fall into some black plastic tubs. Simple.

There were two other parts to the worm gin, and they were the beginning and end of the whole process. Both were rolling

5

drums. The first drum was massive and revolving and its purpose was to cook the garbage to make it even easier for the worms to eat. It was a silver octagonal tube, about twelve feet long by six feet high, that acted as a supercomposter. The other drum was the screener, another long silver tube, which separated the worm poop from everything else (including any unfortunate worms that didn't crawl fast enough—suckers). There were always some items in the garbage that the worms wouldn't eat or at least didn't get around to eating. Turns out worms have eating habits that are about as picky as a four-year-old's.

We spent most of the day putting the system together. With the sun setting, Harry pulled out a bunch of bulky burlap sacks. These were our worms' travel cases. Inside were a million red wigglers, cushioned by shredded paper from the journey's jolting. When Harry opened up the first one, I wasn't quite sure what I was looking at. Inside, mixed with the paper, were what looked like red grapefruits, except that they were quivering. It turns out that when worms are frightened they clump together and curl themselves up into balls. Harry assured us that once they were settled into the worm gin they would be perfectly fine.

To make them comfortable and easier to spread into the gin, we mixed them with cow manure (also provided by Harry, courtesy of his "lawn mower," Betsy) and loaded them into the central hopper. Gradually they started to distribute themselves along the conveyor belts.

Up to My Neck

By that time it was eleven p.m., and unfortunately Harry's delay meant that the garbage was stacked up behind us and we needed to get to it as soon as possible. As Noemi and I drove across campus in the rattletrap truck, I tried to keep her excited by focusing on the big picture—telling her how neat it was to be starting a new business, what a huge effect we could have on the environment if the business model worked, and anything else I could think of. Selling the American dream—with an eco twist.

In fact I was trying to encourage myself as much as Noemi. I was sick to my stomach about the debt! I had spent many sleepless nights trying to figure out exactly how the business would work. I was terrified that the project would fail and I wouldn't be able to pay back the money. I imagined spending three years in my personal equivalent of a Russian gulag: wearing a suit at an investment bank.

Wilcox dining hall had accumulated a dozen fifty-five-gallon barrels—the size of standard oil drums—full of what is known within the composting biz as "postconsumer food waste." The term rolls easily off the tongue. Yet these drums were full of rotting cafeteria leftovers that not even hungry college students were interested in: slop composed of everything from half-eaten sausages to last Tuesday's tuna casserole, coffee grounds and cooking oil, eggshells, and all the noxious, unidentifiable sludge in between. All mashed down by its own weight and gradually turning into liquid. And not only were we facing a virtual mountain of this slurry, but it had been sitting out in the hot sun putrefying for a few weeks now before we got our hands on it.

In the eerie flickering half-light of our truck's headlights we started loading. We had gotten a piece of plywood from Home Depot to use as a ramp to push the barrels up and into the truck bed. Noemi was game, but those puppies weighed upwards of 150 pounds each. We shoved and grappled and dragged a couple of barrels into the truck and decided that would be enough for a start.

As we drove back, the low rumble of thunder alerted us to the gathering clouds in the dark sky. Noemi glared at me as if to say, "I can't believe you actually convinced me to do this." We both knew things were about to get ugly.

I glanced at the worm gin, shiny and new and gleaming, waiting to fulfill its destiny. I smiled at Noemi encouragingly, and we put on our gloves. As carefully as I could, I lifted the lid off the first barrel.

That hot June night, I learned something that I would rather have lived my whole life without knowing. I learned that the combination of heat, time, moisture, and waste is the ideal breeding ground for maggots.

So, upon removing the lid from that first barrel, I was greeted by the most rancid natural odor I have ever had the misfortune of encountering. It was infinitely worse than any smell—feces or vomit or decay—that you could possibly imagine and was complemented by an army of writhing maggots that made it appear as if the moldering sludge were actually alive.

"Just breathe through your mouth," I gasped, throwing Noemi a shovel.

Things quickly went from bad to worse. As if the fact that we were shoveling this shit wasn't horrific enough, the wood chipper had been designed to grind up dry, dead wood—not the greasy cafeteria leftovers of privileged undergraduates. The sludge that had been brewing in those garbage cans proved to be a nightmare for the chipper. Every few minutes or so it would clog. Of course, the only way to unclog the machine was to reach deep down into it and scrape out, by hand, the garbage that had clogged its teeth. And since the teeth were slightly more than an arm's length away, we almost always got just a little bit of that oh-so-pleasant glop on our faces. Once the machine was finally cleared, we'd transfer the vile pulp onto the conveyor belt leading into the cooking drum and start all over again with a new barrel of garbage. And then go back to Wilcox for a few more barrels.

At midnight, it began to drizzle.

We were heaving two more barrels into the truck when we were suddenly caught in a swirl of glaring flashlights. A car door slammed, and an authoritative voice asked, "Just what are you doing here?"

It took me a minute to be able to piece together an

explanation that any reasonable person—much less the campus police—would find acceptable. Finally, I was able to convince the officer of the truth, that the university had authorized us to dispose of the waste from the dining hall. After a lot of yes-sirring and nodding, we went back to the job.

By the time we'd dispatched the police, the rain was coming down in sheets. After a while, Noemi and I were too exhausted and stunned to talk to each other anymore. Harry was long gone. The whole odious process went on late into the night. Understandably, by our sixth and final trip Noemi was already near the end of her rope. It was after two thirty in the morning when, on the slippery wooden plank we'd devised for loading the pickup, the last barrel fell over, spilling the putrid, maggot-infested swill all over her legs and feet.

Noemi staggered a few steps, puked, and quit.

CHAPTER 2

Praise to Marley, Let the Enlightenment Begin

The six months between starting Prince-
ton and shoveling rotting food waste had required quite an
evolution of mindset on my part. Perhaps I was used to it; my
life had begun in the middle of major turmoil. I was born in
1982 in Budapest, Hungary, when it was still a rock-solid
communist stronghold; we had the "pleasure" of learning the
Russian language in kindergarten. My parents were doctors,
but because they refused to join the Communist Party, a
neighbor ratted us out and the secret police promptly confiscated our passports. My dad, mom, aunt, grandfather, and I
all lived together in a tiny apartment in downtown Budapest

near the Opera House on Andrássy Utza—one of those stately flats with tall ceilings that the Communist Party decided to subdivide into the equivalent of project housing after World War II. We had no money; even though they were doctors, my parents made the same as the folks who pushed the elevator buttons in our building. The only additional compensation for delivering a baby or curing some ailment was typically a basket with a bottle of vodka, a few kolbász links, and, ironically, a few cartons of American cigarettes (rock on, communism!).

Life in Hungary in the mid-1980s was no picnic even in the best of times, but then in April 1986 the nuclear reactor in Chernobyl, which was relatively nearby, blew up. This epic environmental disaster greatly compromised the economy and food supply of all Eastern European nations, since they could no longer export food for fear of it having been contaminated by radiation. Tremendous political instability quickly descended on the region, which luckily put enough pressure on the Hungarian secret police to give all of the confiscated passports back to their rightful owners. Ironically they had been right to take them—within twenty-four hours after receiving our documents, at age four, I was suddenly told we were leaving our home. We drove off that night in our Trabant with not much more than the clothes on our backs.

We made it to Belgium and stayed there for a few months before moving on to the Netherlands, where we lived for more than a year with a professor my parents had met at a medical conference. America wouldn't give us refugee status, but Canada did, so we emigrated there. I landed in Canada in 1987, and we moved in with my mother's uncle, who had left Hungary after the 1956 revolution against the Russian occupation.

Though both my parents had been respected physicians in Hungary, they were required to redo all of their training, beginning with internships, to qualify to practice medicine in Canada. Despite the fact that my family basically had to start over from scratch, I grew up happily in Toronto, attending elementary school there and, eventually, Upper Canada College (UCC), an all-boys private high school where our teachers wore their graduation gowns on a daily basis and where inappropriate touching had been only recently outlawed. Don't let the sarcasm mislead you—I had a brilliant time.

At UCC my best friends opened my eyes to the world of possibilities afforded by entrepreneurship. Jake's dad, Michael, had come from a nice middle-class family, worked his way into the concert business, and become the largest concert promoter in the history of rock and roll—he's a recent inductee in the Rock and Roll Hall of Fame—yet he started as a cabdriver. Anthony's father, Don, cofounded Roots clothing. Neither of them finished college; both had simply followed their dreams and accomplished amazing things.

Until then, perhaps due to my experience in Hungary, I'd figured people who had money pretty much had it from day one while the rest of us worked for a living and never got to be very rich at all. Before I met Michael and Don and saw firsthand what they had accomplished, I'd never imagined that such a thing was possible. Suddenly, success on a huge scale was an option for me, too!

When I was around fourteen, I figured out how to design Web sites. The Internet was just becoming popular, and people thought it was a big deal that I could do this, so I wound up making a nice little profit and even had a chance to hire a few employees. That lasted a couple of years, until I met a man named Robin Tator. Robin is an eclectic entrepreneur with more stories than you can believe in one sitting. For example, he got kicked out of high school in Toronto for joining a teachers' union protest, then, unfazed by his expulsion, he aligned with a group of likeminded (and recently expelled) students and they created their own high school. After his academic career he became the top life insurance salesman in Canada, later taking his sales acumen to join a direct cookbook sales business, where he had hundreds of sales reps leaving beautiful coffee table books with the receptionists at random offices at a great deal (90 percent off since they could buy so many) in the hopes that the receptionists would help sell them to their coworkers. And if they did they would get a free one. This worked well until he tried to break out on his own and lost it all on a desert book.

I ran into Robin a few years later when he was working

on an idea for a do-it-yourself Web site called Werehome .com. He started out asking me to lead the design of his Web site and wound up asking me to take over the entire development a few months later.

The Internet bubble burst just when we were going to close the first round of venture capital funding. That was also about the time I was accepted to Princeton.

When I arrived on campus, I had only a few hours to settle in and negotiate with my new evangelical Christian roommate over who'd get the bottom bunk (I lost). The next thing I knew I was playing one of those corny camp name games with fifteen other bewildered freshmen and two overly enthusiastic juniors, in preparation for a weeklong canoe trip. The premise of this trip, known as Outdoor Action, was to ease us nervous and intimidated freshmen into the Princeton culture during the two weeks before classes.

This was where I met Jon Beyer, a computer science major from Maryland who seemed to me the only (other) sane guy on the trip. After the "fun and games" in the gym, we piled into a yellow cheese wagon (school bus) and headed out to the starting point for the trip, unsure what to expect. As we canoed down the Delaware River, passing a multitude of powerboats, factories, and folks floating in giant inner tubes, drinking cans of beer (and leaving them in the river), I started to miss Canada.

Revolution in a Bottle

America is a big land full of people with big ideas, and unlike anywhere else I've been, it is full of people willing to take big risks on these big ideas. It is a land where failure is seen as a stepping-stone, not a tombstone. It is a land where truly anyone—even Hungarian-born Canadians like me—can live the American dream. But, as I discovered on my canoe ride down the Delaware, it is also a hugely polluted land, one where building a new housing development is seen as more important than protecting the forest that stands in its way.

We returned to Princeton and the wonders of freshman week. I later figured out that the real point of this seven-day blowout was not to orient the incoming class, as they'd have you believe, but rather to give senior guys the opportunity to hook up with as many freshman girls as possible without any of them saying those dreaded three words: "I love you." For me, it was also a time when the myth of cheerleaders and football players that I'd seen in movies during high school came to life before my eyes.

Those first few weeks at school, you're bombarded by pitches. Princeton has a million clubs and associations, and they all try to snag as many incoming students as they can (who can resist free labor?). Out of the tornado of flyers, posters, and letters, one in particular caught my eye: an announcement of the Princeton Entrepreneurship Club's annual Business Plan Competition—grand prize $5,000. I pointed this out to Jon, and he was interested, too. This was big money for us. But we needed an idea. We played around with a bunch of nonstarters, from selling photocopiers in bulk to cutting hair.

Pretty soon I was going to classes and staying up till four every night, trying to read the insane number of books assigned to me by each of my five professors. I took all kinds of classes—not economics but things like psychology and Buddhism. That October, a Princeton psychology professor, Daniel Kahneman, was the co-recipient of the Nobel Prize for economics. Kahneman was looking at economics from a psychological point of view, such as asking questions about why and how people took risks or didn't. For instance, if you offer people the choice between receiving $100 this week or $110 next month, they are more likely to take the $100 right away. Or if you and your friend are both making $10 per hour and I asked you which you'd prefer: (a) you both get $15 per hour (a $5 raise for each of you) or (b) your friend stays at $10 and you go to $14 (a $4 raise for just yourself)—which would you pick? Most people choose *b*! I decided I would create an independent major that combined psychology and economics—"behavioral economics."

Also that first semester, Jon and I grew to be good friends, despite how busy we were. I liked him from the start. He was shy and polite—the kind of guy who waits at the corner for the light to change instead of just jaywalking (I jaywalk—although the cops in Princeton did end up giving me a ticket for that a few years later)—and a fantastic computer programmer to boot. He's also a total cycling nut and would eventually become captain of the Princeton cycling team.

Before too long, Jon and I were enjoying the ever-escalating success of the "pre-street" parties we were throwing in my dorm room. By November, our modest get-togethers had grown from twenty people or so to more than one hundred students squeezing into our room looking for that coveted can of Coors Light. During our rapid growth we even had to get the girls next door to open up their room to absorb the overflow of freshmen.

18

When our first official break came around at Thanksgiving, I decided to take three friends on a road trip to Canada, to show them what they'd been missing, living life in "da dirty South" (. . . really the most important thing they had been missing was the Canadian drinking age of eighteen). We took in a U2 show in Rhode Island and then piled into our little Ford Escort and drove directly up to Montreal, where we crashed in a run-down house that some Canadian friends— Jake, along with Steve and Pete—had rented.

In high school, my friends and I had taken advantage of Canada's enlightened laws about the private cultivation of marijuana. That is to say, we were growing it. The most promising of these young seedlings was nicknamed Marley (after Bob—although thankfully she was a girl), and before I left for Princeton, it was decided that Marley, due to the "political climate" of the United States, would need to move to Montreal with my buddies and take up residence there in a dingy basement closet.

On the standard diet of chemicals, artificial light, and water, Marley hadn't been doing too well. Pete's reports on her condition had prepared me for the worst. Still, I was pretty anxious to see her. With an odd smile playing around his mouth, Pete led me to a closet at the bottom of the stairs. With a flourish, he threw open the door and cried, "Check her out!"

I could hardly believe my eyes.

Marley was . . . well, she was glorious. Her leaves were fat and green, and her stalk was straight and thick. This was not the plant I'd said good-bye to a few short months earlier. "What happened?" I asked. "She was nearly dead!"

Pete was beaming. "I changed my approach, about four weeks ago."

"How?"

"Worm poop!"

I chuckled.

"I got a worm box and began feeding Marley worm poop," Pete explained. "She's been off the chemical diet and on a steady path to recovery ever since."

"All thanks to worm poop?"

"Yup. It works like magic."

We went upstairs, where Pete, smiling like a proud father, showed off the secret to his success—an ordinary garbage can, no more than a couple of feet high, lined with black plastic. Inside were trays containing what looked like rich, dark soil along with watermelon rinds, eggshells, and other kitchen slop—and worms. Hundreds of them. Maybe even thousands.

That moment, the proverbial lightbulb went off in my head: we could take people's garbage (a service for which we could theoretically get paid), feed it to tons of worms (which is an environmentally friendly process), get beautiful worm poop (which Pete had already proven was a fantastic fertilizer), and then sell it to the masses! The idea for TerraCycle was born.

We celebrated by inviting Marley's friend, Mary Jane, to the party. She gave us all a little kiss, and we went to sleep, dreaming of poop and profits.

The epiphany in Montreal was serendipitous, since the Entrepreneurship Club's Business Plan Competition was right around the corner—the end of January, to be exact—and frankly we didn't have a better idea to run with.

First, we needed to demonstrate that we could make a profit. We thought that this was the easy part as our raw material (organic waste) had a negative cost. We found out that Princeton was disposing of such waste at a cost of around $50 per ton. Moreover, we discovered that the market for such services (waste management) was *huge*!

I didn't know a thing about writing a business plan, and neither did Jon, so to help us, and to keep the party hopping, we enlisted eight of our closest friends and together began to write a business plan for what we called the "Worm Project." Our model revolved around making a tremendous amount of money by taking in a large volume of organic waste and feeding it to a huge army of worms. Once the worms had done their business, we would sell worm poop fertilizer to farmers and landscapers.

The next step was to set out to see if there were any such businesses already in operation. Surprisingly, we found an entire worm-farming industry (complete with recurring trade shows and its own publications)—yet the industry was in shambles, thanks to a lurid pyramid scheme led by Greg Bradley of B&B Worm Farms, a company he'd started only two years before TerraCycle emerged.

Here's how it worked: B&B would host seminars in small towns, touting the wonders of worm farming. Bradley informed his audiences that red wigglers, the special worms used in vermicomposting, not only broke down garbage at a ferocious rate but also doubled in population every ninety days. This was true. However, he went on to claim that he needed an amazing amount of worms (multiple shipping containers' worth) to fill lucrative contracts he had negotiated in Sierra Leone and with a large chicken farm in Ohio.

Armed with this story Bradley combed the country, looking for farmers who wanted to get rich quick and were willing to spend their savings to invest and grow worms for him. The arrangement was simple. Farmers would invest roughly $30,000 for three thousand pounds of worms (roughly 3 million worms), as well as an additional $30,000 to build the worms a home at their farm. The worm population would double every ninety days, and Bradley guaranteed he'd buy back the increase in stock at the same $10-per-pound rate—to supply those large contracts around the world. Therefore, he explained to the farmers, they would be making roughly $10,000 a month happily farming worms.

Bradley offered a fistful of success stories: David White of Conway, Arkansas, who invested $5,000 and had seen a return of $87,569! Doug and Holly Stark of Peculiar, Missouri, had also invested $5,000 and saw a return of $82,610!

You can probably guess where this was headed. It eventually came to light that there were no large contracts with Sierra Leone (go figure), and the buyers who'd purchased David White's and Doug and Holly Stark's worms were not chicken farmers in Ohio but rather the next string of newly branded worm farmers whom Bradley had talked into starting a worm-growing business. This classic Ponzi scheme eventually netted Bradley more than $29 million from more than three thousand clients—clients who were left high and dry a few years later, in January 2003, when he died of a cocaine overdose.

To this very day, there is tremendous speculation in the worm community over whether or not Bradley did in fact die, or whether he staged his own death and fled to an island somewhere in the Caribbean. We'll probably never know for sure. It turned out that Bradley "died" the same month Terra-Cycle was incorporated. With this melancholy serendipity all possible competition in the worming world had been wiped out by B&B.

The only other competition could theoretically come from industrial composting sites, which make profit by taking in waste, just like in our business model, and turning it into compost to sell to farmers and landscapers. However, composting without worms takes between six and ten months, while worms can do the same thing in a few weeks—*and* in a much smaller space (roughly a hundred times smaller). Also, solid worm poop has a market price almost *one hundred times* that of compost. And the vermicomposting process, as it's called, is virtually odorless (in other words, the noxious odor of rotting food waste that we were shoveling completely disappears once the worms get to it), unlike composting—which has a notoriously hard time getting zoned due to "not in my backyard" folks complaining about

23

the foul odor. Basically, once we got the foul stuff in our system it would stop smelling putrid and come out smelling like damp forest.

Through our research of the worm industry we learned that most people put the worms in trays. For example, the ex-B&B worm farmers, whom we'd enlisted as advisers, used systems composed of hundreds of trays, and tending them required forklifts. The less sophisticated ones, mind you, just threw a bunch of organic waste into a pile on the floor, then dumped the worms on top, waited two months, and finally separated the wriggling masses from the resulting poop.

Clearly the processing presented an opportunity for innovation, and the solution—like many epiphanies—came to me when I was sitting on a toilet. If you think about it, most animals, including the average human, doesn't like to hang out in (or even near) its own feces. A toilet is basically a contraption to take our poop away from us as quickly as possible. One flush and that turd is in another state!

Turns out worms are the same; they tend to prefer hanging out in food, not their poop (discerning little creatures). So after a few random ideas, including putting them on a slope or in a tube, we settled on slow-moving conveyor belts, where a belt would move in the opposite direction from the worms, and at the same speed, to keep the worms in the same place, eating, pooping, and multiplying. Honestly, I was a little jealous.

Praise to Marley, Let the Enlightenment Begin

Two months later, our team had completed a 105-page business plan that carefully laid out how the Worm Project would solve the world's landfill problems by converting billions of tons of organic waste per year into worm poop, all while making money on both ends. One late night in January 2002, we printed the ten copies of the business plan we needed to enter (running out of paper twice). The only thing we didn't realize when we dropped them off was that we'd missed the deadline by one day.

There are more than two hundred business plan competitions in the United States every year, and they all follow the same basic outline: teams are asked to submit their business plans, and if approved by the judges—a panel of venture capitalists and successful entrepreneurs—they are invited to present in person, for typically a strictly enforced fifteen minutes.

The Princeton Entrepreneurship Club forgave us being late and agreed to consider our plan. We waited. The judging wasn't completed until March, and by that time our team of eight had dwindled to three—Zack (one of my four roommates), Jon, and myself. The others were just not into the idea of a career in worm poop, we realized, and had enjoyed the novelty of thinking of starting a business more than actually doing it.

The first round of judging selected fifteen teams

to present their ideas, which ranged from a student furniture exchange to a program that would allow students to instant-message questions to their teachers in class instead of raising their hands.

To our surprise and dismay, it turned out that the judges had only skimmed our business plan and were impressed not by its contents but rather by the sheer weight of its paper. When the dust settled, we found that we'd come in fourth—the only finalist team to finish without prize money. Which is honestly the worst position to be in—sort of like being "the first loser."

Jon, Zack, and I trudged wearily out into the cold winter air that evening, our heads hung low in shame.

Life went on—reading, studying, partying—but I could not get the Worm Project out of my mind. I talked about it with Robin, who loved wacky ideas and was completely into the prospect of selling poop for a living. Aside from our shared enthusiasm, however—and the two thousand worms living in my dorm room in a container about the size of a large shoebox—we didn't know how to make it a reality.

Luckily, Jon couldn't let the Worm Project go, either. Surfing the Internet, he came across an industrial-scale system for collecting worm poop compost, the infamous Harry Windle's worm gin. The second I spoke to Harry, I could tell he was completely nuts, but he was our kind of nut. Harry's system hinged on the same conveyor-belt principle that our idea had, only he took the concept to a whole new level—literally. Harry's worm gin boasted conveyors stacked on multiple levels and could accomplish what we'd imagined in a tenth of the space.

I quickly negotiated a deal with Harry: he agreed to build us a system that could handle the waste from one of Princeton's cafeterias; he'd even do it for half price: a mere $20,000. Not that Jon or I had $20,000, for that matter—but what a deal!

So, even though we couldn't afford the system we began lobbying Princeton to allow us to dispose of the school's dining hall waste during the upcoming summer. We started with the head of the dining service. After seven meetings, he gave his approval, and we triumphantly signed on to take the waste from Wilcox dining hall every day throughout the summer. Then we had to go to grounds management to convince them to give us a place to put the worm gin. You guessed it—seven more meetings.

At the thirteenth of the fourteen meetings, I couldn't wait anymore. School was almost over. I called Harry and gave him the go-ahead to start making the worm gin. By calling Harry and agreeing to buy a machine that I couldn't afford, we put ourselves on the line. Perhaps that was the moment TerraCycle really began.

With two weeks before the end of the term, we finally received official notification from the university. Jon and I

combined our savings (amounting to just over $5,000 . . .
$5,324.18, to be exact) and sent a check for $5,000 to Harry
as a goodwill 25 percent down payment. He said he would
have it ready by the middle of June. Then I called an old
buddy from high school, Anthony, who agreed to lend us
$5,000 of his bar mitzvah money. In the same breath, I
maxed out the credit cards my parents had given me and
then called them to borrow the balance. Within a month, I'd
accumulated the $20,000 we needed.

On a whim, and to make sure Harry was legit, I decided
to drive down to Florida to visit him the weekend before
school was out. I asked Noemi—who'd joined us a month
earlier—to come with me on the trip. We could afford to rent
the car for only forty-eight hours, and it turned out that
Noemi, like any typical New Yorker, didn't have her driver's
license, so I had the pleasure of driving up and down the east
coast in a record forty hours.

On the way down, Noemi and I brainstormed company
names. Some of the more notable ones included Gia Green,
Magic Worm, and TerraPoop. We finally settled on TerraCycle
as we crossed over from Georgia into Florida.

Before too long we arrived at Harry's, which lay in the
middle of a Floridian swamp. Harry proudly introduced us to
his cow, Betsy, whom he'd been employing as an environmentally friendly lawn mower. (The next time we were there,
we ate Betsy for dinner—she was delicious.) We hung out for

a few hours, getting to know one another and talking about the gin, then hit the road again for the twenty-hour return trip home.

Four weeks later, our new friend Harry showed up with our magnificent, brand-new worm gin, and twelve hours after that Noemi quit.

Jon quit his job in Maryland and within days found himself helping me shovel the rotting waste we were now obligated to dispose of.

June was a dark month. In the whirlwind of buying the worm gin and convincing Princeton to let us do our thing, we hadn't calculated for the cost of food or lodging and found ourselves broke, sleeping on the floor of a friend's dorm room during the week, scrounging for meals wherever we could find them at night. As any discerning Dumpster diver knows (and we soon found out), coffee shops and restaurants throw out their food around closing time every night. This means that their Dumpsters are full of amazing finds—ranging from bags of bagels to all sorts of other yummy things. As long as you don't mind competition from your local raccoon, free food awaits!

In the morning, we would get up, pick up the morning's serving of dining hall waste, and take it down to the gin. Chipping and shoveling it into the rotary composter took until the middle of the afternoon, and by six we would have it all fed to the worms. Then we'd eat dinner and go to work on the business. We sent our business plan out to every venture capitalist firm we could find, in the hopes of securing some funding, and received nothing back but a steady stream of rejections.

As the summer wore on, things became increasingly bleak. By the end of July, all we'd really accomplished was proving that the worm gin actually worked (phew!) and that we could indeed produce ample amounts of worm poop. The rest of the plan, however, was a total failure. We weren't being paid to take away anyone's garbage, and we hadn't sold a single ounce of poop.

I remember the night it finally hit me—all too clearly— lying on the floor, unable to sleep, and feeling my stomach turn as I planned what I'd say to everyone who'd lent us the money to finance the worm gin. During a somber breakfast conversation Jon and I had the next morning, we decided to sell the worm gin on eBay and use the money to pay back some of our debts. I resigned myself to working at an investment bank over the next three summers in order to cover the rest.

As luck would have it, Jon and I had arranged to do a live interview about the Worm Project on a local AM talk radio show that very morning. Instead of canceling, we decided it would be a cool way to wrap up our foray into the worm poop business before going back to school in September. So that crisp and somber morning in early August we rolled into the WCTC-AM studios near New Brunswick, New Jersey, in that rented, rusty old pickup. Jon and I told our whole story to Bernard, the talk radio morning guy—from our first aha moment in Montreal to the woes of disposing of dining hall refuse, and the bittersweet joy of producing some damn fine worm poop. The half-hour interview went by in a heartbeat—we walked out with a cassette tape of it in hand and a business to fold.

When we arrived back at Princeton, there was an e-mail waiting in my in-box from someone named Suman. It looked like the kind of e-mail you almost automatically redirect to the trash. However, being in the depths of despair I was open to entertaining anything.

I clicked on it and rubbed my eyes.

All it said was: I WANT TO INVEST. CALL ME.

That night, Jon and I had dinner with Suman and his family at a local restaurant. After eating, we drove down to the south end of campus to show him the worm gin. I explained exactly how it worked, then we stood there looking at it in silence for a while. Finally, Suman tapped me on the shoulder.

"So . . . how much do you need?"

"How much do you have?" My heart was pounding so loudly I could hardly hear myself think.

He smiled broadly. "How's two thousand dollars?"

"That would be great," I said without skipping a beat. "*Really* great."

"Glad to hear it," he said. Then he proceeded to write a check right on the spot.

CHAPTER **3**

Hard Times

Suman's investment wasn't a bonanza,

but it was enough to give us time to take a deep breath and
regroup. Our friend who had given us the floor of his dorm
room over the summer was leaving for the last couple of
weeks before school—as was his dorm room's availability. So
the morning after we cashed Suman's check, we headed over
to a local real estate agent, a "jolly" Irishman who promptly
gave me a lecture for not wearing a suit to our meeting—even
though he still reeked of the bar from the night before, or
perhaps that morning.

In the end we found a basement office suite on Nassau
Street, right across from the university and about a half mile

from the worm gin. There was one central room with a small office on either side of it. The two offices became our bedrooms. Just outside the suite was a bathroom, so we could use the sink to brush our teeth and take "sink showers." Months later when Robin would start coming down to New Jersey to help he would also crash with us in the office. One night at four a.m. (while we were out), in his underwear, he walked in a stupor to the bathroom, only to discover when he got back that he had locked himself out. Being a half-naked middle-aged man, gold chain, thick mustache, and all, in a conservative, cop-infested town like Princeton is a predicament. Luckily our friend found the spare key moments before he convinced himself to break down the glass door.

The office wasn't completely raw space, but it needed some paint and, most of all, furniture. Office furniture was expensive, and besides, since we'd spent most of Suman's money on the rent and security deposit, we couldn't afford to buy anything.

So the day after we took possession, Jon and I walked around campus looking for furniture discards. Sure enough, there was a pile of office furniture outside the offices of the campus business magazine, *Business Today*. We asked the people setting up the office what was going to happen to the furniture, and they said it was going to be thrown away. It was garbage, as far as they were concerned, and they didn't mind at all if we hauled it away. It was natural—after all, we were in the waste management business. Total cost of our office furnishings: $0.00.

Zero was a big number for us at the time. Our staff was zero, our customer base was zero, and our income was zero. Needless to say, our salaries were also zero. When we had time and weren't exhausted, Jon and I looked for seed money, sending our business proposal out to every venture capitalist and investor we could find. The response was still—you guessed it—zero.

What we had lots of, though, was worm poop—bags and bags of it sitting around the office. So, with a little regret and a whole lot of relief, we shut down the worm gin, boxed up all the worms, and stored them in the office. Operating the worm gin was, after all, a hell of a lot of work, and we had only contracted to handle the waste from the dining halls through the summer. But we had proved that it could generate compost magnificently—everyone who used our worm poop was amazed at how well it performed.

A few weeks later there came a letter from a group named Tropika International, based in Toronto. Tropika was run by two men: John, an enthusiastic, fortyish man; and a younger fellow named David, who handled the financial side of the business. Their pitch was that Tropika would find investors for TerraCycle so that I could focus on the operations. That sounded great to me. Other than Suman, this was the first time anyone who wasn't a friend or a fellow student had shown serious interest in TerraCycle. It was a kind of validation that I hadn't had before. They invited me to visit their office in Toronto so we could discuss terms face-to-face. I couldn't wait.

The first visit to Tropika was inspiring. It was a large office with new furniture, very well appointed in every respect. John seemed genuinely excited by the business and the prospect of growing it. He asked me how much money I was looking for—I said around $20,000—thinking mainly that then I could pay off that credit card bill and the money I owed. We opened up a bank account and added John's name to it.

They were even willing to lend us office space for Robin and for Sam, another Canadian, who had heard about the Worm Project and enthusiastically joined the team. Now we really were international, with offices in the United States (Princeton) and Canada (Toronto).

With all this, in the short term we still needed more money—just to pay rent. The most successful gig we had was to bring in my friend from Los Angeles, Grant, to cut people's hair (later I found out that Grant was in fact a hair stylist for a different type of hair . . . something that needs to be manicured when making adult films). There really wasn't any place that students could go to get a really good-looking haircut in Princeton. There were plenty of places for older people, but students went wild for a "celebrity hairstylist from L.A., in for only one exclusive weekend." This was a real marketing coup. We got hundreds of girls and had Grant booked every thirty minutes all weekend. . . . What can I say, it paid the rent.

Most Fridays that semester, we hosted an art party at the office. We found a unique formula that worked like a charm every time we did it. We would get a big piece of canvas, three feet high and eighteen feet long, and hang it on the wall of the office. We'd supply paint in cans on the floor, some beer and snacks and whatnot, and invite a bunch of our friends. We'd suggest to everyone that it would be great fun to fill up the canvas, however they wanted to, whether or not they'd ever painted before. Skill and talent, we emphasized, didn't matter here.

We'd start it off, or someone would, and gradually people would start to have fun. Then an interesting thing happened. Once the canvas was filled, people would start painting one another. Pretty soon all their clothes would be filled. The next thing you knew all their clothes would be off . . . making their skin the canvas. This happened every time! So we had discovered another reason to have art in the office, which we expressed in a simple formula that Jon and I wrote on the wall in pride: ART + BOOZE = NUDITY.

The parties had at least one positive business result, however. One of the regulars was a senior named Hilary Burt, who liked the whole TerraCycle vibe as much as the parties. She started helping out around the office for four or five hours a week. She was such a strong supporter of TerraCycle that she even convinced her father to invest $6,000 in us.

The *New York Times* had done a little article on us in the business section over the summer that called us "a Princeton success story." (The title was "The Employees Really Are Spineless"—everybody seemed to love the worms.) There had been some other local articles and of course the radio program that had brought Suman in. We were now getting inquiries literally from all over the world—Barbados, Hungary, Japan, and the United Arab Emirates. *Inc.* magazine saw some of the publicity and assigned a reporter to talk to us.

Early in the fall, I asked Robin if he was willing to really put some time into TerraCycle, in return for a share of the business. Now that the weather was cooling in Canada with the onset of fall, his ice-cream business was going into hibernation. He would come down every other week, sleep in the basement office, and help put the business on its feet.

Our biggest change was figuring out what business we were in. We took to heart one of the crucial lessons in entrepreneurship (not to mention life): when something isn't working, do something different. We hadn't found anybody who would pay us to haul away their organic waste, and it was pretty clear we weren't going to find anyone. What we had were bags and bags of the best fertilizer on earth.

Worm poop has twice the calcium, three times the magnesium, five times the nitrogen, seven times the phosphorus, and eleven times the potassium of the surrounding soil. Nitrogen is a key ingredient in healthy plants—it promotes leaf growth and assists with protein synthesis and other vital plant functions. But even though it's crucial to growth, most plants are not able to extract nitrogen from any of the naturally occurring compounds that it usually forms unless it is also abundantly supplied with calcium. Worms not only provide extra nitrogen in their poop, they also have a calciferous gland that helps them process calcium. Moreover, worm poop adds busy microbes and bacteria to the dirt, which can be enormously important to the health of the soil. So it's not only feeding your plants, it's feeding your soil. Bottom line: worm poop is some great shit.

We had always imagined that we would sell the worm poop as fertilizer, but now we realized that we should focus all of our efforts on that instead of on making money on the garbage input. Our first attempts seem rather pathetic now: we just put the worm poop in clear plastic bags that we labeled "Pure Worm Poop" in plain black type on white paper stickers we bought at an office supply store and printed with our office ink-jet printer.

The idea was that the customer would simply scoop out the worm poop and spread it around in the garden, just as you would with a bag of planting soil or compost. I would put some bags in the back of my gray 2001 Ford Taurus station wagon (which my parents had given to me that summer) and drive around to local hardware stores and plant shops. I would walk into a store and the person behind the counter would say, "May I help you?" and I would launch into my pitch about how I had a very unique product that I was hoping the store would stock and so forth. Usually at that point the person would cut me off and say that I would have to come back when the manager was there as the salesclerk didn't have the authority to make any decisions.

Eventually, I got smart and started calling before I visited a store, so that at least I would start out talking to the right person. I would go through my spiel, and then I would pull out my sample bag of worm poop. Some people laughed in my face. The more polite ones would suggest that it would be hard to sell "Pure Worm Poop" for various reasons, from the name to the packaging.

Also, despite the fact that worm castings are not harmful and in fact are quite clean, it was clear that people did not want to have much contact with it in its original state, fresh out of the worm. Robin, whose background is in marketing, came up with the idea of making it into a spray, which everyone thought would be more attractive to consumers and therefore the store buyers.

That turned out to be a brilliant suggestion, because not only was it more consumer friendly, but liquid fertilizer has a number of advantages over solid fertilizer. First, liquefying the castings makes them go a lot further (not that we had such a high demand at the time). Second, spraying it on the leaves of plants reduces the possibility of diseases attacking the foliage and increases the amount of nutrients the plant can absorb (since the surface area is so much greater). And on top of all that, some studies have shown that liquid fertilizer improves the nutritional qualities and taste of vegetables.

Making liquid worm poop is not very difficult to do nor does it require expensive, complicated machinery. Basically, you take a plastic bucket and dump some worm poop in it. Then you put in a tube (or several tubes) attached to an air pump. Fill the bucket with water and start the pump so that there's a continuous and plentiful supply of air bubbling through the mixture. The point of the air is that disease-causing bacteria and such don't survive well in air. They thrive in anaerobic conditions, so as long as there's plenty of air going through the tea it is supersafe and beneficial for the plants.

After a day or so, you add sugar or molasses and pour the worm poop tea you've just made through cheesecloth or a nylon stocking and you're ready to go. That is, you're ready to go . . . if you are a home gardener. If you're a business, like TerraCycle, you're ready to put the tea in some sort of container that consumers can use—we had decided to put the tea in the eight-ounce plastic spray bottles that we'd bought, with a different label and a new name—TerraCycle Plant Food. Unfortunately, once you've put the tea in the bottle, there's no longer any air going through it. That means that harmful bacteria start growing in it. And most important, that means, if you're TerraCycle, you have to sell whatever you've bottled up in about twenty-four hours.

That was a problem, but at least now we had a product to sell.

In mid-October, the first *Inc.* magazine article hit the stands—it rocked. There was a big picture of me sitting in front of a pile of worm poop with some of the office graffiti art in the background. Then most of another page was taken up with evaluations of the TerraCycle business plan by some venture capitalists and the editor of *Worm Digest.*

The overall impression was that TerraCycle was a big deal. Our long-term goal was formulated as "To become the dominant alternative waste-management company." And naturally we had offered our most enthusiastic expectations of how the business would grow—$2.5 million in sales in the next year, for instance. In other words, we'd said exactly what any ambitious entrepreneur would say. All in all, it was a fabulous boost. I didn't even mind that three out of the four judges in the article predicted that we would fail. The important thing was that the article raised the profile of TerraCycle.

My hopes went through the roof when John from Tropika called around that time. I hadn't heard anything from him for months, though I knew from Sam that he and David had been helping out with the business plan. Now, all of a sudden, he had someone who wanted to invest. A Canadian who had moved to the Netherlands decided to put $40,000 into our business because he thought it was an unusual, interesting concept and the environment was going to be increasingly important. In fact, the money was already in our bank account. I was ecstatic. John asked me to come up to Toronto again to go over the offer and talk about how to structure the business.

Everything was going our way, so I was a bit mystified when Robin called up on Sunday and suggested that I take John's name off the bank account before I went into the meeting. When I asked him why, he just said that he thought it would be a good idea and that he'd tell me more when I arrived in Toronto. I didn't get there until late, but first thing Monday morning I went to the bank and did as Robin had suggested.

When John, David, and I met, they started off by saying that since we now had other people's money in TerraCycle, we would have to structure the business a bit differently. Of course I knew that we would have to give our investor a share of the business, but John suddenly seemed to be suggesting a great deal more than that. For one, he had decided on a person he wanted to bring in as CEO, someone with some "real business experience." Since I was only twenty and hadn't had any "real experience," that seemed reasonable in a way. However, we would have to pay this new person a substantial salary, and we didn't have any real income yet. Up to this point, after all, we hadn't yet paid anyone anything.

That kind of thing went on for another day or two until it became clear, when I looked at all the numbers, that what was really going on was that Tropika was going to take the company away from us. Robin and I would have to give up most of our share of the company and essentially any right to have any say in the direction or operation of TerraCycle. If it made a lot of money, of course we would do well, too—but it would no longer be our company.

I went home and spent the evening talking to Robin and Sam. It was clear to me that I didn't want to give up the company, and Robin felt the same way. Sam, who had been working somewhat in isolation from us and right beside these guys, was a bit mystified that everything could go so sour so fast. We talked over some ways to work with John and come to a compromise that didn't involve us giving up TerraCycle, but he rejected them all. I had to bite the bullet.

The next day, I told John straight out that we just couldn't really go the way he was suggesting. He was furious, seething—I suspect he never imagined that we would just walk away from the deal. I left his office and went over to where I had been staying that week. David came around and tried to smooth things over, but I think he knew that the differences were so basic that there wasn't any way to go forward. We all tried to put the best face on a train wreck.

Robin had been in that office only intermittently, and Sam cleared out the next day. When I got back to Princeton, I got a screaming phone call from John about the bank account. He went on and on about how I had no right to do that, and it was Tropika's money, and so on and so forth. Meanwhile we had called the investor and talked over the whole situation with him. He was very agreeable and let us keep the money. He didn't care about Tropika all that much, but he liked TerraCycle and what it represented.

As a strange kind of compliment, within a few months Tropika actually reinvented itself as a worm poop company. As CSRplus Vermicast Industries Inc., still to this day it provides both information and products to turn organic waste into worm castings. Its Web site even used to trumpet its association with us. Google the company; it is still out there today.

Unbelievable.

CHAPTER 4

The Carrot and the Stick

As if running a company that could barely

cover the next month's rent and that had a product with a twenty-four-hour shelf life wasn't enough, I had to make a decision about school. All that fall, I tried to run TerraCycle and be a full-time student at the same time. It wasn't working. I wasn't thinking about class even when I was in class. Princeton didn't allow students to attend part-time, so as the semester was coming to an end, I had to make a decision. I decided to drop out.

Another person who provided a key link in those early days was Priscilla, the county solid-waste management officer, who introduced us to the EcoComplex at Rutgers University.

The EcoComplex is about as old as TerraCycle, having been started in April 2001 to "research and educate people about environmentally sound business practices." The EcoComplex is located on the Bordentown Resource Recovery Complex (in other words: "the city landfill"—nice name, eh?). Since it was created to develop "innovative environmental technologies," TerraCycle fit in perfectly. For a while, in fact, we were about its only project (I guess other people didn't like the idea of working on a landfill as much as we did). At the EcoComplex, we set up the worm gin again.

Dr. Bill Gillum (the second person older than twenty-five to join TerraCycle) took it on himself to get the worm gin up and running. Bill was a highly experienced chemist who had worked for Western Electric, AT&T, and Lucent but had decided to retire and find new challenges. We were certainly a new challenge, and we hired him to be what we called "Director of Operations." That meant that he had to make sure things were running, so even with his Ph.D. from MIT and all that experience, he spent the first six months shoveling shit. We didn't really have any employees at that point. We were still depending mainly on interns for the grunt work, but Bill pitched right in.

Despite the many disappointments at not finding investors and the experience with Tropika, we kept entering business contests and won several of them. Our business model had been significantly refined, and we had jettisoned the waste management side of the business to focus entirely on being the best eco fertilizer company. We entered the Princeton Entrepreneurship Club's business plan contest again, and this time we won the top prize. Unfortunately, now that we had an office and people we had to pay, at least occasionally, as well as expenses, we kept on needing money. In the month we won the Princeton contest, we paid off some bills and were down to $500 in the bank.

All that was left was the big gorilla of the business plan contests that year, the Carrot Capital Business Plan Challenge. Carrot Capital was a newly formed venture capital firm that sponsored a nationwide contest with a grand prize of $1 million (in the form of investment capital from the company). Naturally, the competition rose with the size of the prize. In 2003, there were 750 entries. Everything was on the line with Carrot. It was do or die.

Having won seven other contests, we weren't entirely surprised when we were named one of the twenty finalists, which meant that we would have to do our presentation in person in New York City. We stayed up the night before to get ready, refining the presentation, printing it out, and binding it on our Nassau Street office floor. Robin came down from Toronto and on April 26, 2003, a Saturday, we took our PowerPoint presentation into New York City one more time and did our thing at about two in the afternoon. We showed a bottle of TerraCycle Plant Food, though to call it our product was something of an embellishment. It was liquid worm poop in a new bottle with a sticker label I had printed on the office printer the night before . . . not to mention having designed it the night before as well.

The winners would be announced at a dinner that evening, so we hung out in the hotel for three hours until a cocktail reception at the Forbes Building on Fifth Avenue. There was a cocktail party beforehand to announce the *Forbes* Entrepreneur of the Year—obviously not us.

I was wearing my usual casual outfit (jeans and a T-shirt) while everyone else was in typical investment banking getup—suits, ties, the whole thing. Robin and I stood around trying to make conversation, but nobody was talking to us— it was sad. We were incredibly depressed at this point. Everyone was looking at us like we were dirt. At one point Robin nodded to me to go out of the room for a chat. He was thinking the same thing I was. "There's no point in staying here," he said morosely.

"We're out of it. We must be. Nobody's even looking at us. We might as well go home."

"There's one thing, though," Robin said.

"What's that?" I couldn't imagine what he was talking about.

"There's a free meal."

So we went back in, and they called everyone into the

dining hall. Robin and I sat down at our table, which turned out to be in the very back of the hall . . . to add insult to injury we were at the "booby table."

There were the usual kinds of speeches, and the first course, and then they announced the ten teams that had not made it to the next round. Here it comes, I thought.

But no. They got to the end of the list and still hadn't said our name. Robin and I looked at each other with our eyebrows taking off. Those first ten didn't win any money, but everyone from this point on would get at least $100,000. That was a pretty good piece of change. So I spent the next course figuring out how many different ways we could use $100,000. Then they announced the next five. We were still in the running. After the next course, they would announce three more, all of whom would receive $250,000. That was when they served the entrée, which I just couldn't eat because I was so wound up. When they started announcing those three, it was like the business plan contest version of Russian roulette; I was just desperately hoping not to hear our name.

And I didn't.

I didn't even bother trying to eat the dessert, whatever it was. I knew the next name I would hear would be the team that had won a half million dollars. I had no idea who the other finalist was—until their name was called first after dessert. We had won. Suddenly all those people who wouldn't talk to us were giving Robin and me a standing ovation as we walked up to receive the prize. It was surreal. I took the bottle of wine they gave us, and after a little schmoozing, I went back home to New Jersey.

The next day was Sunday, so I called Bill to give him the good news and luxuriated in the thought that we wouldn't have to be spending so much time just raising cash. The only thing that bothered me was that David, Carrot's managing partner, had mentioned something after the awards ceremony about toning down the emphasis on the garbage side of our business. I didn't see the point in that, but I wasn't too worried about it then because there was so much else to talk about. Maybe we could afford an office with windows. Maybe we could have a manufacturing plant. Just maybe I could have a salary!

On Monday, the whole TerraCycle team—we must have been thirty people (mainly friends or "interns")—went into New York City to open the Nasdaq, which was a terrific moment. We were interviewed on CNBC's *Power Lunch* and a couple of other news shows. We were generally feeling pretty terrific about things. I talked with David about him coming to see the office and the worm gin at the EcoComplex. He agreed that was a good idea since Carrot would work up a deal sheet about the specifics of the offer and how it would be paid, and so forth. The prize, it turned out, was really just a term sheet—an offer of funding from Carrot.

That next week, David and some others came down and

looked over everything. At one point, they took me aside and started to talk about their plans for TerraCycle. As he'd suggested at the dinner, they really weren't too interested in the environmental benefits of converting garbage into worm poop. They did see a big opportunity in the organic nature of our product. They must have figured that organic fertilizers and plant food would be a fast-growing market for consumers, which was what we figured, too.

Then the next week, they brought me into New York and talked some more about how they wanted the company to develop. They would bring in their own team to take over everything about the business—manufacturing, production, sales, marketing. They would make me the public face of the company, but it would just be a company that sold an organic fertilizer. They told me I would become famous and rich, and I wouldn't even have to work that hard at it. I said that I didn't think that was necessarily the best way to go forward and went back home to Princeton to think things over.

Eventually they sent me an e-mail that laid out essentially what they were going to offer. It boiled down to two major items: lose the garbage side of the business, and lose the entire current staff. Not only did I think that was unfair to the people who had been so generous with their time and effort, but it didn't make any sense to me. The garbage-based business model was what made TerraCycle distinctive and had attracted so much attention and support.

I called David and ended up saying, "If that's the way the things are going, I don't think we'll be able to come to terms." He wasn't too happy, but at that moment he just hemmed and hawed. Later that week he sent a five-page letter about what a terrible decision I'd made and how disappointed he was and how with Carrot Capital, TerraCycle could be everything, and without Carrot Capital, it would be nothing. I didn't respond to it, and I heard nothing more from him, so in fact Carrot never really made us the offer that was the prize we had won. I think he was just shocked that anyone would turn down the money. By that time, I was becoming an expert at it.

I was also becoming an expert at living on the brink. After all was said and done, we still had only $500 in the bank. There weren't any more business plan contests to enter, at least for that year. We could try making money the old-fashioned way—by selling a product and getting paid for it—but we still didn't have a way of putting vermicompost tea into production or delivering it to stores or the consumer in any form that would be attractive.

So the day after we turned down Carrot's proposals, we all met in the basement office on Nassau Street and tried to figure out what the hell to do next. It was a moment of desperation. Robin dropped into a creaky office chair with a weak spring and nearly flipped over. He glared at me.

"It's garbage, dude, you have to watch out for that one" was all I could say. We were all agreed that Robin's idea of vermicompost tea was the most consumer-friendly way to deliver the fertilizer. Bill was working on stabilizing the tea so that we could assure stores that it would last on the shelf.

Most important, how were we going to get the bottles we needed to hold the tea to take to the stores to bring in the cash? We had everyone in the meeting, including our advisers via conference call—it was a "Hail Mary" moment. I asked Robin how many bottles we could buy with our last $500.

"None," he said. "They won't let you buy anything unless you buy in bulk. The minimum order is something like a thousand dollars. Probably more."

Over the phone, Howard (one of our advisers) tossed in an epiphany: "Why not temporarily grab used bottles from people's recycling?"

A light went off in my head. "Wait, that's a brilliant idea." They all looked at me. "We have a product that is made from garbage . . . why not package it in garbage?"

"Well, it's garbage, for one thing," Bill said sarcastically.

"Look at the furniture you're sitting on," I said. "We picked it up out of what was essentially the garbage pile. It works perfectly well." Robin pointed at his chair. "Well, almost perfectly well."

"How are you going to get them?"

"We'll pick them out of recycling containers."

"We're just going to be filling them up with liquefied worm poop, after all," Robin pointed out.

"Look, this is just a temporary solution until we can afford to start buying new bottles again. We'll stick on a label and start selling them tomorrow," I said.

"You're going out tonight?" Bill looked dubious.

"We need the money. You gonna join us?"

After the meeting broke up around midnight, I got some extra-large garbage bags and gathered together four of the interns. Out we went to look through recycling bins for any kind of plastic bottle we could get our hands on.

For those of you who don't know the town, Princeton is one of the more posh suburbs you might ever want to live in. It hadn't occurred to me that anyone would object to us going through recycling bins and sorting out the plastic bottles, but after we'd been collecting bottles for a couple of hours, suddenly we heard police sirens, and a couple of patrol cars pulled up, lights flashing. Several Princeton cops slowly pulled themselves out of the cars, waving their flashlights in our eyes. "What do you think you're doing?" one of them demanded.

I couldn't help but remember Wilcox Hall's food waste and the campus police wondering if we were stealing garbage. I tried to explain what we were doing and why, but the police wouldn't understand. They were not happy, to the point where it actually became a little hairy. "We'll let you go this time," they said, "but if we catch you doing this again, we'll have to lock you up. It's against the law to go through people's garbage." At least they let us keep all the bottles.

We went back to the office. The other interns were coming in with their collections, so we dumped them all out on the floor and started sorting. Between the five of us, we had assembled a pretty substantial number of bottles. I expected that we would have all different sizes and shapes, so I was very surprised to see that there were only four sizes of bottles: two liters, one liter, a half liter, and twenty ounces (591ml). But what was an even bigger surprise was that for any given quantity, the heights, the bases, and the thread of the cap were all identical. The only real difference between them was the contour of the bottle.

That may not seem like something that could provoke an epiphany, but it did for me. What was important about the similarity of the bottles was that they could be run through high-speed bottling lines. And that meant that TerraCycle Plant Food could be mass-produced in used soda bottles! Sure, at that moment, we were going to pour vermicompost tea into the bottles by hand, using jugs and funnels, but in the future we would be able to run the bottles through a bottling line and crank out thousands and thousands of bottles of plant food per hour. What we had seen two hours earlier as a temporary stopgap solution suddenly became *the* solution.

Revolution in a Bottle

———

At that moment TerraCycle Plant Food was born. Ironically, because we had turned down the investment money ours became the first fertilizer in the world (and it's still the only one today) that is made entirely from and packaged entirely in waste (except the label)!

The idea of finding value in what people are willing to pay to get rid of is one of the fundamental backbones of Terra-Cycle. Think of it this way: There are three major components of any piece of waste (such as a plastic bottle), the material (plastic PET), the form or shape (a bottle), and the intention (to hold a liquid). In the recycling model, the material has positive value, because it can be sold as a commodity. But in order to do that, you destroy the shape and intention and reduce the material to a form that is useful for making something new. So the shape and intention have, in a sense, negative value.

Reusing something is inherently better (both economically and environmentally) than other solutions as you value all three aspects of the object: material, form, and intention. Upcycling is the second best, where you value the material and form of the waste but not the intention. Next is recycling, where you value just the material. These three waste solutions: reuse, upcycling, and recycling are all cyclical approaches where the material can go around and around as long as people collect it. The two popular noncyclical solutions to waste (both negatives) are landfilling (where you don't value any aspect of the waste) and waste to energy, or incineration (where you only value the caloric or energy value of the waste). Both of these processes can happen only once, and both release toxins into the environment while wasting all (in the case of landfilling) and some (with incineration) of the value inherent in the waste.

Almost every time you buy something today, you're buying an array of goods. Suppose this book is giving you a headache and you need to buy a bottle of aspirin. In addition to the tablets of aspirin you buy, you're also buying a piece of cardboard that packages it, the plastic it's wrapped in, the bottle that holds the tablets, and a little piece of cotton. You're probably also being awarded a plastic bag as a bonus from the store you bought it from. You may not be able to think of a way to use each of these items, but you probably can find a use for some of them. When you do, you're unlocking the power of waste.

Back to bottles. It turns out that every year, Americans discard (not recycle—just throw away) more than 200 *billion* soda bottles. The amount of waste is astounding, and the impact on the environment truly staggering. However, there's even a further problem. Between 1995 and 1998, the plastic used to make bottles (polyethylene, usually called PET) increased by more than 50 percent, replacing other materials like glass—mostly because of the introduction of the twenty-ounce soda bottle. At the same time, recycling of this type of plastic *declined* nationally, from about 40 percent in 1995 to 25 percent in 1998. The problem for recyclers is that these containers are both bulky and lightweight—they take up a lot of room in the truck but they still don't weigh very much. And weight is the way recyclers get paid. "If you have a truckload of plastic, you're still not carrying much," says Rosalie Green, an Environmental Protection Agency recycling specialist.

That night, of course, we were focused on more immediate problems. We took the bottles, cut off the labels, rinsed them out, and, using our trusty funnel, filled them with liquid worm poop and slapped on a sticker we had recently printed on the ink-jet printer in our office. The next morning we started going to small retailers in our area. One of the interns at the time, Ryan, sold the first ten cases out of my station wagon. We were on our way and starting to make sales!

CHAPTER 5

The Big-Box Approach

The irony of our first product, liquid worm poop in a used soda bottle, was the raw economics. Today the cheapest way to make a bottle is to use virgin plastic; if you want to go more environmentally friendly you may consider adding recycled content (which will raise your price). If you want to go even more eco-friendly you may consider plant-based plastic, but with that choice your cost will go up again. The status quo paradigm is simple: the more eco-friendly you want to be, the more it will cost you and in turn your customers. This doesn't just go for packaging, it applies to all "good" or "eco" monikers from "fair trade" to "organic." However, if you reuse a used bottle you are paying for only the plastic (not the shape); by definition it will always be the cheapest and most eco-friendly choice.

During this time I was driving around New Jersey, visiting local retailers to sell the fertilizer, and for the first time we started to see some steady, although very tiny, income. In addition, we were constantly giving away free samples to get people to try the product. Which meant that we needed a steady supply of bottles. Since raiding Princeton's recycling bins was not an option, according to the local law enforcement authorities, Robin and Bill began investigating the large-scale recyclers, but very often their bottles had been crushed and couldn't be salvaged. Eventually we would find dependable sources of high-quality used bottles, but that was still years in the future.

It came to me one day that there was an entirely different way to get quality used bottles (something we later discovered could apply to all waste): ask people to collect them before they put them in a trash or recycling bin. After all, so far we had survived in large part on the volunteer help of interns. People were willing to work for free when they felt they were doing some good or learning something valuable. I had the idea of using the local schools to help us collect bottles. We would go to the local schools, do an assembly about recycling and reuse, and ask the kids to collect bottles for us.

The Big-Box Approach

We'd give them a giant box, and every morning they could bring in their quality used bottles and throw them in the box. Moreover, as a little incentive, we would pay the schools a very small fee for each bottle they collected, and of course we'd pick up the bottles for free.

We first tried out the idea not at a school, since it was the end of the school year, but at a church not too far away from Princeton. The pastor there was very interested in TerraCycle, but he was still a little skeptical, especially when it came to asking his young parishioners to collect bottles. After a few meetings, I convinced him to let us try, and so one morning I stood up in front of about fifteen ten-year-olds. I had brought everything I could think of to sell the idea. We had a television with a VCR to show a video about TerraCycle, and we brought some worms and some of the garbage that we fed them. We brought in the big box for the church lobby. I evangelized for fifteen or twenty minutes about recycling and reuse and how they could make the earth a better place by giving TerraCycle their old soda bottles.

When I was done, I asked if they had any questions. One little boy raised his hand. "How does a worm poop?" I have to say I hadn't prepared for that particular question. It was all about the worms for them. They loved touching them; they asked about what they ate, how long they lived, and how big they got.

Whether it was the worms or the environment, the

"bottle brigade" was a terrific success. The kids were excited by the idea of TerraCycle, but maybe even more they were excited at the idea that they could go into a store and see a bottle that they personally had collected. They were also earning money that their school or church could use. It was a win for everybody involved.

By the end of that year, there were thirty groups regularly collecting thousands of bottles per week for us.

Meanwhile, the disaster with Carrot Capital turned out to be a huge bonus for us. Though we had turned down the money, we hadn't lost the sizzle. Carrot's interest was a signal to others that there was something real here, and I was able to bring in some small investors that kept us going. In May, as a favor for one of these small investors, I went to the annual meeting of a company named Universal Display, which had nothing to do with TerraCycle and sounded like something from a science fiction story.

It was the last thing I wanted to do—and on my way down I got lost for almost an hour trying to find the venue. So I walked into the meeting room and took a seat while Universal Display was presenting its goals for the next year. It wasn't really the most exciting presentation I'd ever seen, which is maybe why the person next to me started to chat. He asked me why I was there, and I said, "Oh, I'm really just doing a favor for a friend. This really doesn't have much to do with my business."

"Well, that's very nice of you. My name's Martin Stein. What's your business?" I proceeded to tell him the story. He kept asking questions, and after about ten minutes, he took my hand and asked, "How much money do you need?"

I was tired and wasn't up to figuring out how much Martin was really likely to invest, so I just said, "Five hundred thousand dollars." Why not, I figured, he'd probably laugh.

But he just said, "Okay, I'm in. Consider me your partner." We shook hands, and he said he'd call me the next day and visit. I was still, naturally, skeptical.

But he called the next day and came down to see the business—that is, the office where I slept and worked. Bill gave him a tour of the EcoComplex, and evidently Martin asked Bill if I would be a good investment. I don't know exactly what Bill said, but the next day the money was wired to the TerraCycle bank account! Which just goes to show that you should never dismiss any opportunity, no matter how unlikely it seems on the surface. Over the coming years, Martin was always ready to help. When I called him up, he would say, "How are things going? How much money do you need?" More than that, he became part of the company family. Today Martin and Edith Stein have transferred their significant ownership of TerraCycle into a trust that will ensure that all of their proceeds go to various charities that are close to their hearts.

Meanwhile Doc Bill, when he wasn't making worm poop and fulfilling orders, started a huge test to determine how effective TerraCycle Plant Food was. Huge is perhaps an understatement. It involved acres of plants in a greenhouse.

There was a funny thing about the EcoComplex: since it was government-run we always had chain gangs come through to help clean up the place. Robin, being a smoker, realized that since inmates couldn't smoke we could get a whole day's labor with a simple promise of a single cigarette. Since Bill needed more people, we promised one of the inmates, Ron, a full-time job when he got out of the can. He even slept beside the worm gin in a tent.

For the experiment, Bill kept records on six hundred plants, vegetables, and flowers, each of which had to be precisely watered and measured every day for the entire summer. Then they all had to be pulled up to measure the root growth and a dozen other things that would show that TerraCycle Plant Food was actually an effective way of stimulating plant growth. It was a complete success. At the same time, he had to keep the worm gin going and keep it supplied with organic waste, which we got from various places around the state.

Bill and his team concluded that our worm poop was actually better than typical commercial plant fertilizers. That is, not only did it increase root growth and protect against disease, it also had amounts of nitrogen, phosphorus, and potassium that would make it comparable to other consumer fertilizers on the market.

It was at the end of this experiment that Ron disappeared. Turned out he'd stolen a single shoe from a store near the EcoComplex. After serving his time for the great shoe heist, Ron became a greeter at our local Walmart.

Up to this point we had followed the advice of just about everyone we talked to in regard to how to build your brand in stores: You go to the little stores and build up your brand, and then you go to a bigger store and a bigger store, and finally, when you've really established yourself, you might go to a major big-box retailer. Oh, and if you go to Walmart they'll destroy your price and kill you, 'cause that's what they like to do at Walmart—they eat little suppliers for breakfast!

So we began with the "start small" model, and it was a pain in the ass. The local stores would buy a case here and a case there. Then we'd have to ship them cases individually, invoice individually, get them to pay us individually, and deal with any problems that arose individually. What was really annoying was that we never really had any idea if the product was selling. They might reorder when they sold out, and then again they might not. Moreover, to even be given the opportunity to sell to a small retailer you typically have to go through a distributor like Ace Hardware that will take 5 percent to put you in its catalog, 10 percent for this, and 2 percent for that—oh, another 3.5 percent for the thing they forgot to mention at the beginning. The whole system is a hindrance to growth.

We weren't growing fast enough—barely bringing in $1,000 per month. We had to drive and pick up the soda bottles in my Ford Taurus station wagon—it could hold exactly 854 bottles—then clean, fill, and label the bottles manually. It was incredibly labor-intensive—every aspect of it. Without Martin's generosity, we never would have made it.

Meanwhile, TerraCycle needed something to boost business. The model clearly wasn't working, so we tried a bigger situation—the lawn and garden trade shows. We'd have to sit in these places—these huge convention centers—and people would walk up and down the aisles and you'd have to pitch each and every one of them who walked by your booth, and in the end they might order a case. "That's cute," they'd say. "Maybe next year." Or the best was: "Could you give us a free case and we'll see if it sells and if it does maybe we'll buy more?" It was brutal. I hated every second of it. I wanted dot-com growth rates, but we were growing like a nice little organic consumer products company—slow and steady, hoping for word of mouth or guerrilla publicity or a miracle to jump-start sales.

The shows didn't build up the business, and we always spent more money traveling—San Francisco, Houston, Chicago, Detroit, Racine—and setting up for the shows than we ever made. I remember in particular a show in Las Vegas that was on two floors and we were in the basement. We had spent $15,000 on the booth, the mandatory union worker help, and the travel. It was three days long, and in that whole time two people passed us. I wound up sleeping on the floor for half the show. Robin was there with me—at one point I woke up on the floor and looked at him and said that this was the most screwed-up way to do this. We were going to stop. We were going to go to the biggest stores and beat down their doors with a battering ram.

Big-box retailing came onto the scene in the 1950s, and today those stores are by far the leaders in each industry. In other words, today, if you sell to Lowe's, Walmart, and Home Depot, you will reach over 75 percent of the entire lawn and garden market in the United States.

So naturally, flying in the face of all odds, Robin and I started to call the big-box stores—Walmart, Home Depot, Lowe's, all of them. It was really hard to get through. Nobody picked up. So we kept calling—every hour on the hour. We even changed what phone we called from and left only one message a day. After thirty-five days, a buyer at Home Depot finally picked up the phone and gave us thirty seconds to make our pitch. I told him, "We have the world's most eco-friendly product—it's made from and packaged in waste—and best of all it's cheaper than the competition." Then he said it sounded interesting but we should talk to So-and-so in a different department. So-and-so passed us off to someone else, and someone else passed us off, but finally we were passed to the dot-com person, the one who handled the company's Web-based business, who gave us a meeting.

Of course this was dot-com, so it was really for peanuts in comparison to the company's retail stores' sales, but we went crazy about the opportunity anyway—we brought worms and plants grown with and without our product; we had the PowerPoint presentation; we wouldn't let them say no. They ended up placing an order. They weren't risking very much. But it was our first big order, a pallet of product. So we flew back from Atlanta and went directly to the EcoComplex to help Bill fulfill the order.

The bottling line, at this point, was still fairly primitive (handheld plastic funnels). We had a dishwasher to clean out the bottles. When they were dry we put the labels on them with a contraption made of four paint strippers. These are things that basically look like hair dryers but deliver a lot more heat. We had bought a bunch of what are called shrink-sleeve labels. You would slide a label onto a bottle and lower it into the middle of these four paint strippers, which were arranged like the points of a compass, but pointing upward. You had to wear a glove or you'd burn your hand, but the hot air would shrink the label securely onto the bottle. Perfect, if you did it right. Then we'd fill the bottles, screw on the tops, and box them. The boxes, of course, were overruns (misprints). I remember we had a lot of Dasani boxes at one point. Of course we had to break down the boxes and turn them inside out so that the Dasani label wasn't showing. Then we'd stamp them with a rubber TerraCycle stamp and, bang, there you were.

In the end, we shipped as much in that one order as we had shipped in the previous six months. All while we were still calling Martin for modest additional investments on a regular basis.

This is another fundamental of green business: unless you make the product equally economical for consumers, they aren't going to buy the product. Sure, some products that are "organic" or "environmentally friendly" have gained a certain cachet that allows them to build their brand at a higher price point, but that's only true for a niche market—if you want a high-performance car and have the money, you will buy a BMW rather than a Taurus or a Volkswagen. But this applies to only a limited group of consumers, not to the mass market.

I have had intense arguments about this with people who

run environmentally conscious companies. For instance, Jeffrey Hollender, who founded Seventh Generation, once said with pride that his company wouldn't sell to Walmart (although it does so today), and he made a number of cogent arguments as to why consumers are (and should be) willing to spend that extra 5–20 percent on greener and organic products.

Unfortunately, his arguments work beautifully in an ideal world, not the everyday world of the average American consumer. Seventh Generation is one of the largest manufacturers of eco-friendly cleaning products in America, with annual sales of over $100 million. While this is a highly respectable achievement, this growth has been achieved over twenty-five years and it is unlikely that Seventh Generation sales will ever come close to those of a single SC Johnson brand like Windex.

My disagreement with Jeff, and with many others who make green products, is that it is not enough just to offer a green choice at a premium price; the goal is to make green products at a competitive price. I believe strongly that if Seventh Generation offered its products at the same price as Windex, it would be significantly larger today—perhaps even bigger than Windex.

I've given hundreds of lectures since I began TerraCycle and many times I ask the audience this hypothetical question: "You walk into your local supermarket and see two displays for different brands of the same product. One holds the organic, eco-friendly, fair-wage version of that product. It costs $1.05 a bottle. Next to it is a normal version of the product processed with artificial chemicals and harvested by workers paid slave wages (it also happens to be shipped here from China). This version costs $1.00 a bottle. Assume that both versions give the same performance. Who would buy the one that costs $1.05?"

Every time I ask this question, roughly 5 percent of the people's hands go up. It's as if every audience is reading from the same script. (I also count myself in the group that wouldn't pay extra.) I've even asked this question at a recycling retreat in Vermont, where the majority of the audience wore no shoes on their feet and plenty of dreads on their heads. The result was the same.

I then ask the following question: "What if the two products were the same price? Which one would you buy then?" Again the audience seems to have been given a script—100 percent of the audience (there has never been an exception) raises a hand in support of the eco-friendly version. It seems fairly clear to me that everyone wants to buy organic, eco-friendly products, but it's equally clear that they don't want to pay more for them.

Environmentally conscious economists often point out that with our current form of capitalism most companies are not paying for the cost of the capital they are withdrawing from the earth. Oh, they pay people to extract the minerals, cut the trees, deplete the soil, and pump out the petroleum, but that's it. It's as if the earth were an enormous unlocked vault of infinite resources that can be turned into things that can be exchanged for money. Everyone can take whatever he or she wants as long as they pay carfare to get to the vault and haul away the stuff. And most companies don't pay for the costs of discarding their waste, or for subsequent health or environmental impacts from their products. These "externalities" are passed on to society.

Once natural resources are exchanged for capital, they get "used," and usually after one "cycle" of life we throw them into landfills or burn them. From our experience with packaging worm poop in used soda bottles we saw the value in this garbage. Properly reused, upcycled, or recycled, almost all forms of waste can continue to cycle and especially be exchanged for money.

CHAPTER 6

And Then It Clicked

The HomeDepot.com order wasn't a big one in terms of numbers, but it was huge in showing us the benefits of major retail. It would have taken us much more time and effort to put together the same amount of sales with individual stores.

The success with HomeDepot.com quickly started to open doors. Now we were able to make contact with people at some of the other big stores, and at the beginning of 2004 we hit the road, trying to meet with as many as we could: Canadian Tire, Zellers, Stop & Shop, Walmart Canada, QVC, Publix, Whole Foods, and many, many more.

It was a thrill. Not that we were making any meaningful

money, but the idea that we were selling to Home Depot fueled our excitement. If our business model focused around sales, the future appeared to depend on scaling, and big box was the clear pathway.

As we grew our sales and operations, it was obvious that we needed more space. For one thing, the three of us couldn't continue to fill orders from the EcoComplex by hand, with paint strippers and funnels. We needed a staff, we needed storage, we needed machines—we needed a factory. Even the ever-generous Martin Stein couldn't support the kind of expansion we were envisioning. So we would have to do a large part of it on our own.

As a way to bring on much-needed help during the end of the school year in the spring of 2004 we went on a massive intern-recruiting spree led by Alex, our lead intern. We held weekly meetings in the office on Nassau Street, where we'd pitch people on the exciting world that TerraCycle had to offer. Ten to fifteen people would show up almost every week. We promised them everything we could think of—from a mansion to live in to a butler to feed them—none of which we had at the time. By the time we were done, we had thirty-five interns ready, eager, and willing. With a month to go, we still didn't have a home to house the students for the summer, office space for them to work in, or that elusive butler.

I had a budget of roughly $1,500 per month to pay for a place to house more than thirty-five people. Princeton wasn't even close to an option. Going north only meant higher prices. So our only option, really, was going south. Which was what Trenton had been doing for decades.

If you had to find a human equivalent of discarded soda bottles, it would be America's inner cities: there are no jobs, schools are inadequate, property values are low, and so on. Trenton, New Jersey, is one such place.

At one time, Trenton was one of America's proudest and most bustling cities, with a long history. It was the scene of George Washington's first victory in the Revolutionary War, when he crossed the Delaware River at night on December 26, 1776, and surprised the British mercenary troops in Trenton. The city was the new nation's capital for a couple of months in 1784. It remains the capital of New Jersey.

During the early 1900s, Trenton was a major center of the American Industrial Revolution, housing such companies as Roebling Steel, the company formed by the builders of the Brooklyn Bridge, and many more. It was one of the country's fifty largest cities and a booming manufacturing center for steel, rubber, wire, rope, linoleum, and ceramics. The city adopted the slogan "Trenton Makes, the World Takes" in the 1920s. The 1931 *Industrial Directory of New Jersey* proudly listed four hundred businesses with five or more employees in Trenton.

You'd be lucky to find forty now. Manufacturing started to decline in the 1950s, and people started to leave the city. By 1960 it had dropped off the list of America's one hundred largest cities. Savage race riots followed Martin Luther King's assassination in 1968. In the 1970s, heroin took over the economy and the society while gangs, especially the Bloods and the Crips, took over the streets. The Bloods are a major part of the cartel that controls heroin in Trenton, as well as a substantial part of the statewide heroin traffic.

All this within ten minutes of one of the richest zip codes in America—Princeton.

By the time we started to look at houses in Trenton, the population was 85,000, and maybe a third of all the buildings in the city were abandoned. There was no artistic area, no place that would be a basis for rejuvenation. The property values had plummeted. Trenton was (and remains) the fourth most dangerous city of fewer than 100,000 people in the United States.

All this made Trenton the best real estate option we could find. Although no new houses had been built in Trenton (outside of low-income housing) for fifty years, there were some extraordinary houses left over from Trenton's glory days. Ultimately, I found a grand old house on Greenwood Avenue, which had once been called "Millionaires' Row" fifty years earlier. It had seven thousand square feet and a dozen bedrooms.

When I moved in I distinctly remember seeing something

And Then It Clicked

I couldn't figure out. From the street sign on the corner nearby hung two bandannas, one red and the other blue. That was my introduction to the Bloods and the Crips. We were on the border between two gangs that were sworn enemies. In fact, one of the previous owners of my place had been the heroin kingpin of Trenton. We found out later that two years prior there was a murder in the house right next door to mine, which was used to traffic heroin, and once, while I was away, bullets were shot through my bedroom window. Not because they were shooting at us; we just happened to be in the line of fire.

We moved into the house just when the school year at Princeton was ending, which was a bonanza for us. Most students at Princeton live on campus, but they have to furnish their rooms themselves. When they graduate, they generally just put the furniture out on the street to be thrown away; we were able to furnish the entire Trenton house with discards from Princeton. The house had been modernized a bit by the previous owner, who had used it as a medical clinic, so we didn't have to repair the interior. What we did do was turn it into a place where everyone could have some fun, since it was impossible to leave the house without running into drug dealers or crack whores.

We even found that butler we had promised and his specialty turned out to be fried chicken and fruit smoothies. During that first summer, we turned the basement into a combination poolroom, movie theater, and keg room. As you can imagine, it was used very heavily. As a funny side note, years later when I sold the house I found an entire family living in the basement. They'd been there for what must have been at least a year . . . they had sleeping bags, a stash of food—all the trimmings you needed for basement squatting. They had been feeding themselves by cutting out the copper pipes and selling the material. I guess everyone in that house was in the recycling business.

Since there was only one shower in the entire house, and it always ran out of hot water before everyone could use it, we had to schedule showers on a rotation—and the last unfortunate intern had to clean out all the curly little hairs that congregated by the drain hole.

Breakfast was pretty much a free-for-all, and then we'd carpool in to work. About half the team would go to the office on Nassau Street, while some went to the greenhouse to shovel worm poop or bottle and label orders. We also had a team working on a lawn service—unfortunately, it never quite got off the ground, given the competition from more established (and better equipped) companies—not to mention the interns' weakness for hijinks on the customers' properties.

It was a wonderful and exhausting ride. When I wasn't traveling, I was supervising—sixteen hours a day—which isn't easy when everyone is your peer.

And Then It Clicked

For all the difficulties, the interns made a huge difference that summer. In order to move the TerraCycle Plant Food off the virtual shelves at HomeDepot.com, they called everyone they knew—their friends, their families, the media, local stores, garden clubs—anywhere and everywhere they could think of. That summer, TerraCycle Plant Food became the fastest-selling plant food on HomeDepot.com!

That made it all the more urgent that we find a factory. We researched the properties around Princeton and found them to be completely out of the question due to their prices. But as soon as I saw the prices we could get in Trenton, we realized that was where we wanted to be. Not only because Trenton offered the best space for the price, but also because that was where people needed jobs. So at the end of the summer we took the risk, bought a building on New York Avenue in the northeast part of Trenton, and moved out of our basement office in Princeton. Mind you, we had no orders beyond HomeDepot.com's.

The factory we found was on a city block, with one L-shaped building and a second rectangular one. There was some office space in the front at the bend of the L, two large open rooms on either side of that, and a loading dock in the back. It might not sound like much, but it was perfect for us at the time. There was room for the plastic swimming pools that held the worm poop tea, room for the bottler, room for everything. In fact, it looked huge—after all, we had been doing production out of a one-hundred-square-foot space in the greenhouse!

Of course, it was full of old junk from the previous business: there were a hundred huge metal tables, bindery equipment, and more than fifty derelict trucks on the property.

We were moving into a poor area afflicted with gang violence—and let's face it, we were mostly white Princeton students. Somehow we had to make a peace treaty—or at least a nonaggression pact—with the neighborhood. So we decided to capitalize on another problem that faces our communities—graffiti—and create value, social and environmental good, from it.

Our factory was dilapidated and ugly, so we put the word out that people could paint our factory whenever they wanted. Most people think of graffiti as something like garbage as it creates negative value when someone defaces buildings and other structures. Moreover, they pay to have it removed, like any piece of trash! For the artists, this meant that society was out to destroy their means of expression. So when we bought the factory in Trenton, I got in touch with some local artists and asked them to bring their crew around to paint the building. The response was amazing—the graffiti artists transformed the outside of the building. And since that day our building has been repainted every month with brand-new art. For free!

And Then It Clicked

In the meantime, we had played out our string of big-box store meetings, at least for that season, and had a consistent set of no's. HomeDepot.com was still going strong, but we didn't have any other orders in sight—just one last meeting, with Walmart Canada.

We had been calling Walmart constantly. Finally, at the beginning of the fall, someone over there picked up the phone. We probably made contact because the buyer just couldn't stand to hear our message on his machine anymore. We set up a first meeting in Bentonville, Arkansas, in one of those little meeting rooms that Walmart is famous for. We made our first pitch, accompanied by the plants (with and without our fertilizer) and all the other paraphernalia we could carry there (including worms). The buyer seemed impressed and suggested that we talk to Walmart Canada in Toronto. This was the big moment. Everyone told us that no matter what, it wouldn't be more than a fifteen-minute meeting. Even if that buyer liked us, fifteen minutes was the absolute tops. Five minutes if he didn't.

When we walked into the meeting—me in a green and tattered John Deere hat and Robin in his khakis—we both felt that the Toronto buyer was ready to show us the door at the very first opportunity. He was not exactly hostile, but his attitude made it perfectly clear that he was just meeting with us so he could tell us to drop off the face of the earth.

We had asked Bill to give us three of the biggest, juiciest

tomatoes he could find in our gardens in the EcoComplex. When we walked in, we didn't say anything, just put the tomatoes on the table and sat down. The buyer looked us over and finally asked, "So what are the tomatoes for?" He wasn't allowed to accept gifts from vendors, which a poster in the meeting room clearly reminded everyone.

Robin said, "We wanted you to see what an amazing job our plant food can do on vegetables. Aren't those the most beautiful tomatoes you've ever seen?" The buyer looked non-committal. "And the other reason is that, if you don't like what we have to offer you this morning, you can throw the tomatoes at us."

That broke the ice. Thirty minutes later, he was still fasci-nated with us. He loved the whole idea of a product that was made of waste and was packaged in waste and especially that it wasn't at a premium price. He looked at us as if to say, "I thought I'd heard everything, but I was wrong." He liked us, and he liked what we were trying to do.

As we were getting ready to leave, he picked up the toma-toes and held them, as if he were weighing them. He said, "How much do you think these tomatoes weigh? I'd say this is about two pounds of tomatoes, wouldn't you?" I sort of nod-ded, wondering what he was getting at, but then he reached into his pocket and pulled out a five-dollar bill and gave it to me. "Thanks for the tomatoes," he said. "They look good."

All we could do was go home and wait.

The media kept helping us in surprising ways. During the summer, a Canadian television news magazine, *Venture*, began filming what would become an hour-long documentary about TerraCycle.[1]

Then, just before Christmas, *CBS Evening News* ran a national story on us. Introducing the segment, Dan Rather said we were "proof that the American dream is still alive." They gave us two and a half minutes and said "the product is proving to be remarkably effective." The reporter, Jim Axelrod, ended the segment by saying that the story of TerraCycle "is a reminder about following your dreams. The pot of gold at the end of the rainbow may require dealing with a ton of crap."

The program also reported that we had landed deals with Home Depot and—Walmart. And we had. Not two weeks before, Walmart had placed a massive order for every store in Canada. The Canadian CBC television crew was actually there filming when Robin received the call.

---

1 You can still view this documentary if you search on "terracycle beginning" on YouTube.com.

CHAPTER 7

The Walmart Order

Getting the Walmart order was probably

the biggest thrill up until that point in time for TerraCycle. It wasn't a dinky dot-com order, it was serious—100,000 bottles, worth more than $250,000 to us. That order alone was four times bigger than our combined sales for all of 2004. Not only was it big financially, it was big for the future. We had a chance to impress the biggest retailer in the world.

There was just one catch. No, there were a dozen catches. We had an empty, dilapidated, inner-city factory. We were still trying to clean it up and get it ready for the worm gin and the brewing equipment and the tea vats and the bottler. We only had one worm gin to make the poop, a couple of six-foot tubs, and one rented bottling line—which didn't work all that well.

We had no staff and no equipment, no way to make the thirty thousand gallons of worm poop tea that the order required, let alone bottle it within the time frame we had. On a good week at the greenhouse in 2004, we made maybe a thousand gallons a week. Which didn't include bottling and labeling and everything else. The entire order was due to be shipped no later than mid-February, which gave us two months to quadruple our production, just for starters. For that we would need more people, and it was the beginning of the Christmas season. My few remaining interns were leaving for the holiday, and we were running low on cash. Very low.

The thrill was amazing, as were the problems. We didn't have enough bottles, and we couldn't make enough worm poop ourselves. Once the reality hit, it was gut-wrenching. We'd sold to Walmart without having our infrastructure in place.

Should we have waited to go to them until we had all the machinery and inventory we might need? What if the orders hadn't come in—we would have been broke, and without the energy boost that comes from getting something like the Walmart order. It was truly a chicken-and-egg scenario, and I didn't see how erring on the side of caution would have been a better choice. I had assumed that if we did get the order, then we could figure out how to fulfill it. Be careful what you ask for.

The Walmart Order

Getting the bottles was Robin's task, and it nearly drove him nuts. Maybe even worse, it threatened the core of TerraCycle. When the Walmart order came in, everybody but Robin and me wanted to switch to new bottles. Bill and all the rest of the team thought we should just go out and buy new bottles. We didn't really have enough money to do that, but then we didn't have any money to do anything. It wasn't the money that bothered me, it was the idea of going back to the normal way and dropping the very innovation that had saved us the last time we were almost broke.

We weren't entirely being obstinate about that, either, since we had seen how powerful the idea of making and packaging a product out of waste was. Once you started to dilute it, I thought the magic would be lost.

On the other hand, we were not entirely sure how many used soda bottles had come in from the school program over the past year. It was almost impossible to tell. At one point we had filled up all the space that was available in the greenhouse—imagine a room about fifty feet wide by one hundred feet long, filled to a depth of about three feet with used soda bottles. How were we supposed to know how many bottles there were? We didn't have any time to waste, so we began with the bottles from the schools, and very quickly it became clear that we weren't going to have close to enough.

We then visited every recycling center near Trenton. No luck. As a general rule, recycling centers crush all the bottles they receive because all they care about is the plastic, not the shape. For the recycler, a bottle provides plastic polymer, which is valuable. It also has a shape, which has negative value to the recycler. The shape is garbage, and the recycler will pay to have the shape taken out of the product—that is, a recycling center spends money destroying the shape to get to the valuable polymer.

But what if you also value the shape and intention? We were prepared to haul away the bottles from the recycling centers and pay the centers the same amount they received from their usual buyers, and the centers would save money by not doing their normal processing. It was a win-win situation: we'd get uncrushed bottles, and they'd make the same money with less work. Even today this is the cheapest source of bottles in America!

At the time none of the recyclers were ready to change their processing routines just for us and, as far as anyone knew, just for that order. We were getting desperate. Just a few days before we would be forced to buy new bottles, we discovered the benefit of living near a bottle-bill state like New York. That is, in a bottle-bill state people can turn in their bottles and get back the five cents per bottle they paid in deposit.

So what's different about these state-run centers? *They don't crush the bottles!* Instead they sort them and then send the bottles to recycling centers (which do crush them). At the

The Walmart Order

New York Recycling Center, huge trucks come in from all around the state with enormous loads of bottles. They dump their loads onto a conveyor belt, which leads to a machine that separates the plastic from metal.

This was our salvation. We met with the director of the recycling center and asked him if we could take all the twenty-ounce bottles off his hands. We told him we would pick up the bottles as they came in and buy them for the price he normally got *after* the center did its processing. At first, he was reluctant. It was something new, and it meant changing his system, and nobody likes to do that. The one drawback to our approach is that, initially, it's almost always the harder way to go. We have to invent new logistical processes to make it happen.

Finally, the director grudgingly said we could have them as long as we did all the work. "Oh, and you'll have to provide all the gaylords," he said, and he turned back to his desk to make some notes.

Robin said, "Oh, sure, no problem." I mouthed, "Gaylords?" to him, but he just shushed me. Turns out they are actually cubic yard boxes used in factories.

The final thing was equipment. The first big problem was tanks. We needed fifteen five-hundred-gallon tanks to make enough liquid worm poop to stay on schedule. But since we were doing this entire order during the Christmas/New Year's season, no equipment manufacturer would make anything for us. Every custom tank shop had a lead time that would kill our order: eight to ten weeks.

This was my problem to solve. What object was ready to order and could hold at least five hundred gallons of water? First, I ordered some aboveground swimming pools, which came fast but didn't last. Every single one resulted in a worm poop tsunami at our factory (with me in it). Eventually, I discovered horse-feeding troughs. They look like enormous children's swimming pools and are built to stand up to heavy use.

Once that was solved, we fired up our paint strippers and got to work—we labeled the very first thirty thousand or forty thousand bottles that way, until our newly acquired heat tunnel showed up.

At midnight on February 4, we officially started the big push. We worked fifteen days straight, seven days a week, twenty hours a day. We spent many nights sleeping in the factory taking naps on the front office floor.

We finished in mid-February, one day early, and collapsed.

After we shipped the Walmart order, publicity in Canada exploded. There were articles in all the major newspapers and business papers. CBC's hour-long documentary about us, ending with Robin's call to me about the Walmart order, was broadcast just as we were finishing up the order.

The Walmart Order

On top of all this we had fantastic luck with our timing. In 2004, the City of Toronto enacted a very controversial bylaw intended to encourage homeowners to avoid using synthetic chemical products to kill lawn weeds and bugs. By 2005, about seventy Canadian cities had passed laws that either banned or restricted the use of pesticides for lawn care.

TerraCycle Plant Food fit perfectly into the new awareness of environmentally friendly products. The Walmart spokesman, Kevin Groh, told the *Toronto Globe and Mail* that TerraCycle Plant Food would be "something we're not tucking away in a corner of the store." We were the subject of dozens of news articles, and suddenly there was interest from all kinds of stores that had never picked up the phone before.

Since we were broke again until Walmart paid us—which wasn't going to be for another month or two—we hit the road for more investment. Martin Stein, as always, contributed substantially, but thankfully other new investors also joined the party, and by May we had raised $1.5 million. Just as important, May was the end of the school year, and we had a new wave of interns coming into the Trenton house.

The money and the new interns arrived just in time. We sent them out to visit every Walmart store in Canada—from Halifax to British Columbia—to teach the associates about our product. They did a terrific job, and soon we were selling incredibly well.

Then another up: our big-box hunt bagged the biggest game in the fertilizer industry, a meeting with Home Depot USA. In April 2005, I was able to convince Eric Smith, an adviser at the time, to get me into a meeting with the main fertilizer buyer for Home Depot, John Fuller. As usual, everyone told me that it would be a fifteen-minute meeting at best.

I showed up in the lobby of Home Depot in Atlanta in my usual outfit. This was the first time Eric and I met face-to-face, and I could see he was shocked. After looking me up and down he told me not to say anything, that he would do all the talking.

That meeting, like that first one at Walmart, lasted an hour—and Eric never said a word. Fuller was as fascinated with the model and with the presentation as everyone else was. In fact, so was Eric. Four months later he quit his job and came to TerraCycle to be vice president of sales.

Home Depot agreed to test our poop in stores in New Jersey in August 2005. That year, we increased our sales by more than 500 percent and finished the year with $450,000 in sales.

Our sales didn't grow in a steady, gentle upward grade. We would get a big order, fulfill it, catch our breaths, wait, perhaps wait some more, and then we would get another big order. We worried constantly that we wouldn't have enough product to meet the demand of the big-box stores or perhaps we would have too much and our cash flow would crash. We had chosen growth as an end in itself; scaling created new opportunities and challenges, each requiring bigger solutions.

In addition to needing more equipment, Bill was always looking for new sources of worm poop. We called every worm farmer we could find to see if they would sell us their poop. It turned out that a lot of them had been caught up in the old B&B Ponzi scheme. Naturally, they were more than happy to finally find a buyer for their castings. One farmer in the South was particularly well stocked.

But the problem was that each lot of worm poop had a slightly different composition. Bill ended up developing a secret recipe from a combination of different types of worm poop. He had to mix them, test them, mix them again.

A funny thing happened around this time. We got calls from attorneys at both Coca-Cola and PepsiCo saying that it wasn't legal for us to take their distinctive bottles and use them to hold another liquid (even if it wasn't a beverage). In other words they claimed to retain intellectual property rights over their waste.

After a number of conversations we now have the only license in the world from both Coca-Cola and PepsiCo to package shit in their distinctive shapes.

Luckily, everything we did that year seemed to work.

In June 2006, *Inc.* magazine did a cover story that called us "the coolest little start-up in America." It became one of the best-selling covers for *Inc.* that year. "At the moment, Terra-Cycle seems to have everything going for it. And yet, looking at it today, you would never guess how often the company has come close to failing. On each occasion, however, an angel appeared in time to rescue Szaky and his project. In the end, TerraCycle proved to be the company that refused to die—and a case study in the power of a big idea."

A month later, Zerofootprint, an organization that aims to help people measure the size of their carbon footprint on the environment, declared that ours was the only product they had surveyed that has substantially no negative effect on the environment.

Between the publicity and the visibility in the market-place and the new money, our sales went through the roof—going from $70,000 in 2004 to $1.5 million in 2006. The factory that had seemed so huge when we walked in was now beginning to look small.

Then in early 2007 we landed Target, Whole Foods, Kroger, Walmart USA, and a number of other big accounts. We launched new flavors of worm poop: orchid and African violet, concentrated lawn and garden fertilizers, potting mix, and even seed starter. Since one poops different poop when one eats different food (just think back to your latest exotic travel), we could alter the nutrients of the products by getting farmers to feed different waste to the worms. We were on track for more than doubling sales again to $3.5 million. We were taking off!

It seemed like we had finally found the perfect track, until . . .

CHAPTER **8**

suedbyscotts.com

It was like a nightmare that you couldn't

wake up from. On March 6, 2007, Scotts Miracle-Gro, the largest plant food company in the United States, delivered a lawsuit against us in every possible way. First it came by e-mail. Then it was hand-delivered by a messenger. Then it came by registered mail. It felt like it just kept coming and coming and there was no way to stop it. Had a carrier pigeon showed up with it in its talons I would not have been surprised. The 173-page document said that we were falsely advertising that TerraCycle Plant Food "outgrows the leading synthetic fertilizer" and that our packaging—what the business calls our "trade dress"—resembled that of Miracle-Gro too closely.

The suit was not the first time we had heard from Scotts. In 2006, the company's lawyers had notified us that they had concerns about our packaging and our advertising. We were a little surprised—in fact, we were quite surprised that Scotts Miracle-Gro knew we even existed—but we responded right away that we were willing to work with them to address any concerns they had. We did not have the stomach for going up against this company, and we figured we would be able to come to an agreement. We had gone ahead with a new round of financing, and the signs were good that we would meet our goal of $2 million. In fact, I was expecting to be receiving an offer—and possibly even a check—that very day.

Now, Miracle-Gro is an extraordinary company, one of the great success stories in American business. In fact, it has a trajectory that I only hoped TerraCycle could one day emulate. It is the story of how vision, creativity, determination, and hard work can pay off. It went from being a local operation basically in one man's backyard to being a $3 billion business.

Miracle-Gro really turned into a success thanks to a public relations expert, Horace Hagedorn. According to a DVD biography of Hagedorn that his family produced and made publicly available, Hagedorn was so excited by the possibilities of Miracle-Gro, the product he was promoting, that he took on more and more responsibility for the operation of the company. Eventually he bought out the owner and became the head of Miracle-Gro.

Miracle-Gro's main competitor was a larger company named Scotts. But Hagedorn was not going to let Scott's size stop him. He personally produced a series of commercials, with the craggy-faced actor James Whitmore, that directly compared the effectiveness of Miracle-Gro to its Scotts competition. The ads were so good that Scotts finally came to Hagedorn and offered to merge the two companies.

The new company gradually became the preeminent lawn food company in America, and it has tenaciously defended that position. As *Advertising Age* noted, "With a roughly 59 percent market share, Scotts dominates its business like few other brands." Ours wasn't the first company that Scotts had sued when it felt that a company was improperly trying to imitate some aspect of the combination of factors that had brought Scotts to the top of the heap. "Any claims about our product's effectiveness—we take them very seriously," said a Scotts spokesperson. "I think anyone who is starting and growing a company would understand. It's common sense, Business 101." Maybe the spokesperson meant I should have stayed at Princeton and graduated.

We had not had the slightest inclination to misappropriate any of Scotts's characteristics. Frankly we wanted to differentiate ourselves from them in every way. We thought of ourselves as the "anti-Miracle Gro."

Revolution in a Bottle

It seemed to me that worm poop in a used soda bottle with "worm poop" printed in large letters on the front would not be confused with bright blue powder in a glossy printed box. I agree that we used green and yellow as part of our packaging, and I can only point out that as the colors of the sun and grass, they are widely used by a number of other U.S. fertilizer companies. It's sort of like how toothpaste packaging (both Crest and Colgate) is white and coffee packaging brown. Still, I was prepared to change the colors before the suit and in fact did so after. Indeed, there are a number of things I'd like to say in praise of Miracle-Gro that I am barred from saying by the settlement.

When the lawsuit hit (and hit and hit) my desk, I have to say that I was scared. We were just making our way into the big stores and sales were terrific. But I knew that a prolonged lawsuit could stop us in our tracks. On the one hand there was the cost, which could easily run up to $3 million if it went on for a long time—and a few years is not uncommon. There are all kinds of costs that go into fighting a lawsuit. You have to hire local counsel in addition to your own legal team. You have to provide copies of just about every piece of paper and e-mail that is in or has gone out of the office (in a process known as discovery), giving the plaintiff the opportunity to see if there has been any concerted effort to imitate the plaintiff's products or packaging and the like. This is certainly a crucial part of the legal system, but it can be expensive, not only in materials but especially in the staff time it takes. The costs can easily become so great that a small company can go out of business.

Another problem, and one of the most difficult to fight, is the effect it has on the staff. It's incredibly unsettling and distracting for people—they can't help but worry whether they will have a job at the end of the day, and that's depressing. And if we started missing our shipping dates, we'd lose the credibility and trust we were starting to build up with these tough retailers.

So there were all kinds of reasons for me to be worried. It was incredibly difficult telling the people in the office. I sent out an e-mail with the basic facts, but then I went around to everyone individually and tried to reassure them that we would do the best we could for them and for the company. The last thing we wanted to do was fight this to the bitter end. What we wanted, in fact, was a short, sweet resolution.

However, I think anyone who wants to start their own company or be part of running a company needs to realize that probably some kind of make-or-break situation will hit you before you have things working the way you want. There's never a good time for a lawsuit or a flood or a strike or any of the other things that can spell the end for a small company. You won't be able to predict it, and you won't be able to prepare for it—because you just don't know what it might be. The only way to prepare is to make sure that you're ready to bounce back when something knocks you to the floor.

What is amazing, though, is that in the course of bouncing back you may discover strengths you didn't know you had. Or, as in our case, you may find that the fight itself is an advantage. I can say with some confidence now that if Scotts hadn't sued us, we wouldn't be doing as well as we are.

So I was disappointed that Scotts had decided not to work with us, and naturally I was very worried about what might happen. The first thing was to make sure that no one made any untoward public remarks about the suit or Scotts, so we decided that only three of us—me, our marketing director, Barry, and our publicist, Albert Zakes (twenty-one years old at the time)—would speak for TerraCycle publicly.

Albe, as he prefers to be known, had only come to the company six months before, and he almost didn't. The previous fall, we had put a help-wanted listing for a publicist on Craigslist.com. Albe was an environmentalist who had been working for a public interest research group in Colorado, where he had gone to college.

During our first interview Albe didn't seem a perfect fit—since he had no direct experience in publicity—and we said thanks, but no, thanks. But then he wrote me a long and impassioned letter about why he wanted to work at Terra-Cycle and what he could bring to the job that other people with more experience would not. He was so committed to the idea of TerraCycle and so enthusiastic that I had to believe his passion would make up for his lack of experience. So Albe was our point person, and the point only got sharper when Barry, his boss, left for another job.

In addition to our staff, I had to let our prospective investors know about the suit. I had no idea whether they would decline to continue the process, wait until it had played itself out, or just walk away.

What about our customers? Would they be wary of dealing with us because of the suit? I'm sure that some were, but not all of them. Around that time, I had to go to a sales meeting for suppliers for Home Depot Canada. The media had been invited to this particular one, and *Maclean's*, one of Canada's most enduring and popular magazines, did a colorful story on the meeting:

> Around 2 p.m., the room shifts to a state of heightened alertness. All eyes turn toward the main entrance, where a svelte blond has appeared. It's Annette Verschuren, president of Home Depot Canada. Like dolphins at feeding time, the salesmen all angle for some bit of attention. Soon, Verschuren's gaze falls on the rumpled plant-food salesman. "Tom Szaky!" she exclaims, leaning in for an air-kiss. "Have you seen our new *Eco-Options* magazine?"
>
> "Absolutely," says Szaky. "It's great."

"You have anything new to show me?"

Szaky hands her a plastic bottle of his new spray-nozzle lawn fertilizer. "The spray nozzle— nice touch," she says. "Any innovative products, Tom, you should always consider test-marketing them with us." Verschuren inclines her head at an underling. "We should do an interview with Tom for the *Eco-Options* magazine." Then the executive gives Szaky one last look and says, "You really should come to work for us some day."

Embarrassing as the article was, I was relieved to discover that our major customers continued to deal with us as they always had.

Nonetheless, we had to find a way to fight back. It was obvious that we couldn't outlawyer Scotts people. They had deep pockets and were clearly prepared to stand their ground. We would run out of money before we could beat them in the courts. So that wasn't an option.

We were back on TerraCycle's home ground, so to speak. No money and no power. For anybody born after 1980, the answer in such cases is obvious: the Internet. We started a Web site, suedbyscotts.com, that was intended to get our side of the story out. It presented the facts of the two companies, such things as our relative sizes, pictures of the Miracle-Gro trade dress and ours, what we had said in our advertising and why, and the like. It had both the Scotts complaint and our response.

But a Web site is no good unless people know about it to go there, so we had to get media attention. We thought about hiring an outside PR firm, but in my opinion PR firms are more in the business of getting a monthly retainer and less in the business of getting you press.

So we did it ourselves. In fact, Albe was eager to do it, because he felt that the "big guy versus little guy" story would be a very strong angle for journalists. The headline of the release drove home the point that we were a "Small, Eco-Friendly Organic Company Started by Students." We pointed out that our bottles were recycled, collected by "children in communities across the land," and that we donated five cents per bottle to a nonprofit of their choice. We said that if we went under, inner-city jobs would be lost. And we directed people to the Web site.

Hey, we weren't trying to be evenhanded. We wanted to give the media a gut-grabbing story that had plenty of angles for them to work—and it was all true. Many journalists are overworked, and if you can give them a prepackaged story, you're golden. Most press releases are boring and long and don't really frame the story in an effective way—and sometimes they avoid it altogether. A killer press release is one that a publisher can print almost word for word, with quotes

105

and photos, if it chooses. But most of all, it's all about the headline. The headline will make or break your release.

Naturally, the release went everywhere, but the first responses were with our core friends: environmental groups, schools, and the vast range of environmentally conscious groups on the Web. The bottle brigade program helped terrifically.

At the end of March, Philadelphia's Wissahickon Charter School became the two-thousandth school to join the bottle brigade, and we agreed to supply enough fertilizer to keep the meadow in front of the school green. Some schools near Atlanta had to use a trailer to send us their bottles because people were donating them in such huge numbers. We had collected nearly a million and a half used bottles.

What made the bottle brigade important was that it put our name in hundreds of local papers around the country. Just about every time we started in a school, the local paper would do a story on us. And it gave us allies in communities all over. All in all, TerraCycle's name was more visible than it had ever been.

So we thought we had a good story, but we still had to sell it. Writers get hundreds of e-mails a day and may not read your press release. So you have to call and get them on the phone. Once you're on the phone, you have to care about the story and be passionate about it in order to make them care.

The *Wall Street Journal* wrote that our "overall company sales for the four weeks since the online campaign launched surged 122 percent from the immediately previous four weeks. Last year, the company's sales increased 31 percent in the same period. Meantime, TerraCycle's main Web site, which averages about a thousand visitors a day, has spiked as high as thirteen thousand, according to the company."

We weren't exactly celebrating, but the response to the Web site and the increased sales had improved the morale of the people on the production line. Yet, we were hardly out of the woods. As the *Journal* article pointed out, "no amount of public appeal can help TerraCycle escape the realities of litigation. As part of the discovery process, Scotts has asked for extensive documentation from TerraCycle, including everything relating to product development, contracts with retailers, strategic business plans, as well as details about 'the composition of the materials consumed by the worms.'"

Still, though, we also wanted to get a story on one of the national newswires (Associated Press or Reuters). The Associated Press has a bureau office in Trenton, and reporters there had done a story about the founding of TerraCycle a couple of years earlier that really increased our visibility at a time when it was still pretty low. We sent them the press kit, we e-mailed, and we called and called and called. No response. Albe, who was suffering through serious on-the-job training, didn't have any connections there, and we didn't have a fully equipped publicity contact list, either. It was like beating our heads against a stone wall.

Finally I said to Albe that he should just go down to the Trenton office and make them listen to him. We didn't really have anything to lose, after all. So he did.

He walked into the AP building, and of course there was a security guard there. Her job was basically to keep out everyone who didn't work there. And there was Albe, looking like the postcollege kid he was and carrying plant food and a bunch of literature from us. It was no go. Albe chatted, suggested, cajoled, wheedled, and finally pleaded with her to let him see somebody. A reporter, an assistant, anybody. Nothing.

Finally, it was time for the guards to change shifts, so a new guard came up and asked what was going on. "Who are you from?" she asked. When Albe said he was representing TerraCycle, the new guard said, "Oh, yeah, my sister uses that on her flowers. She says it's terrific." She turned to the first guard. "Let's let him in." And they did.

He pitched the story to an AP editor, who, like most people who hear our story, was fascinated with the business model, the product, and the personal stories. Albe's commitment to TerraCycle carried the day; the AP did a story, and now we had a truly national media campaign—all without spending a dime.

Ironically, the AP story made it into the *Columbus Dispatch*, Scotts's hometown newspaper. It called us "the little green plant-product company." There was also an article in the *Columbus Business First* that began, "It's no longer a big deal when Marysville-based Scotts Miracle-Gro Co. sues. With hundreds of patents and trademarks to defend, lawyers for Scotts are kept working pretty busy." Then it described our Internet-based defense, mentioned the Web site, and concluded, "The basic strategy, it seems, is to shame Scotts into withdrawing its lawsuit. We'll bet worm poop to corporate jets that's not going to happen."

Well, that depends on your point of view. The legal wrangling went on all summer. During that time, we closed our third round of financing for $2 million. Those investors didn't seem bothered by the suit. We vastly expanded the product line, adding plant food for roses, tomatoes, cacti, and tropical plants, as well as offering new sizes.

At the same time, the bottle brigade program was expanding by leaps and bounds. The kinds of groups were also spreading across the board, as well as what they were collecting for. A Little League team in New Jersey started collecting bottles for new equipment. A school in Ohio began collecting bottles as a way to raise money to save an orangutan habitat in Borneo. In Delaware, they were recycling to raise money for the Delaware Autism School. The Djole Dance and Drum Company in North Charleston, South Carolina, collected bottles to contribute to fighting AIDS in Africa.

Local newspapers almost inevitably did a story about whatever group in their area was collecting bottles and why.

109

The result was an incredible synergy whenever we introduced TerraCycle Plant Food anywhere around the country. In July, the Kroger supermarket chain tested our product in stores from Nevada to Ohio, and there were dozens of articles in every state. The combination of the suit, our product, and the bottle brigade brought us a level of publicity and visibility that was probably worth every penny—and there were a lot of them—that we spent on our legal defense.

In September, those costs finally ended. We came to an agreement with Scotts.

So after six months of sound and fury, what had Scotts gained by its suit? TerraCycle was now much more recognizable across the country, and enormous numbers of environmentally concerned gardeners and bloggers were aware of TerraCycle. Many said they would stop using Scotts and switch to TerraCycle Plant Food just because they felt the suit was unnecessary and unfair. We had been the subject of more than 30 million media impressions, including five articles in the *Wall Street Journal*, two in the *New York Times*, and articles in the *Chicago Tribune*, the *Boston Globe*, the *Los Angeles Times*, and the *San Francisco Chronicle*, as well as pieces on the BBC World News, and many, many more. If we had had to pay for that kind of attention, it would have cost easily more than $5 million.

We finished 2007 at $3.3 million in sales, up more than 100 percent from the prior year. We had national distribution in Home Depot, Walmart, Target, and a number of other major retailers. We were in hundreds more stores than we had been in at the beginning of the year. The bottle brigade was at work in thirty-seven hundred locations across the country. While the lawsuit was raging, we opened a round of investment for $5 million and closed within a few weeks of opening it.

What is interesting is that just as Scotts was trying to check our encroachment on its business model, we were once again revolutionizing our business model. We were pleased with the growth of the plant food products, but I became more and more interested in other ways of applying the TerraCycle model—of finding new ways to use things that other people will pay you to dispose of. Could the model be applied to any other kinds of waste? How about *every* other kind of waste? What were the limits, if there were any?

CHAPTER 9

Why Can't Everything Be Made from Waste?

In the first four short years of its life, TerraCycle had been a constantly evolving idea. After that "Aha!" moment with Marley in Montreal, the company had been about waste management. We would undercut other waste haulers because we would use it to feed worms rather than building a modern landfill—which is a complicated, highly regulated project.

Then we saw the elegance of using waste from a dining hall to feed worms whose waste would be our primary product, a highly effective plant food. From this, we uncovered a fundamental thing that ultimately defined our perspective on all future activities: that what other people considered waste could also be considered a raw material.

In looking at waste as an entirely modern, man-made idea, I stopped viewing garbage as garbage and instead slowly started to see it as a commodity. A commodity with some very unique characteristics: it has negative or very low value (typically people pay to dispose of it), it is always a by-product of some other function, it is all around us, it is created in almost every part of our lives, and there is a tremendous amount of it (more than 5 billion tons per year around the world). Since 1960, the amount of waste generated in America by consumers alone has nearly tripled, to more than 250 million tons per year. That's almost one ton per person. It's no surprise that America's biggest export (by weight) is waste. And, just as everything dies, everything becomes waste.

So much waste has been wantonly discarded in the oceans that there is an accumulation of floating plastics the size of Texas slowly swirling in the Pacific. This gyre has been variously dubbed the Asian Trash Trail, the Trash Vortex, or the Eastern Garbage Patch. Not only does 25 percent of all plastic waste end up in the ocean, but there are in fact six gigantic garbage gyres on our planet's oceans that, due to the plastic breaking down into smaller and smaller toxic bits, have the consistency of plastic mush continuing many meters below the ocean's surface.

And we were hitting a wall with TerraCycle Plant Food.

Why Can't Everything Be Made from Waste?

Even with all the new line extensions we were offering (various flavors from tomato to African violet to cactus fertilizer), the simple fact was that the organic plant food market, especially the liquid plant food market, is quite small. It's a tenth the size of the solid fertilizer market, which is a tenth the size of, say, the home cleaning product market. If we were going to become a billion-dollar company, we would need to apply our model to products beyond plant fertilizers.

It was time to reinvent TerraCycle yet again. Instead of focusing on making plant food from waste, we would strive to make all kinds of consumer products from waste. Our first step in going beyond worm poop still kept us in the lawn and garden category. And it started with an internal question: was there waste we were creating that we could use?

After making the worm poop tea, we were left with a lot of "used" worm poop. Sort of like the tea leaves that are left when you brew tea at home (except much, much more). We were, in a sense, throwing away our tea bags—but our tea leaves were still useful. (Yours are, too—you can throw them in the composter.) Although, with purpose, many of the concentrated nutrients leached into TerraCycle Plant Food, the used poop was still full of great stuff. So we used the used poop as the main ingredient of our seed starter and our potting mix. Both were well received, but we hadn't really leapt out of the poop.

As our focus broadened, we were on a constant lookout

115

for ways to transform garbage into viable products. An idea arose when I visited one of our investors, Rich, who owns a vineyard in Napa Valley. One of the most important tools for making great California wine actually originates in Africa. Since both America and Europe lack a plentiful supply of domestic oak, wine barrel makers typically purchase oak in Africa and ship it to France, which has a long tradition of wine barrel construction (cooperage). There the oak is hand-coopered into gorgeous fifty-five-gallon wine barrels and shipped around the world, notably to Napa, where it is used to ferment grapes into wine. It's no wonder that the barrels cost nearly $1,000 each!

Winemakers prefer oak barrels to reusable stainless steel barrels, since they add a flavor to the wine that is particularly delicious. But once the wine is drawn off, after their first (and only) use, these barrels are thrown out! The wine, after all, also affects the wood, and when it is exposed to air, various chemical reactions occur that would throw off the taste of new wine. So the wine barrels become waste, albeit of a particularly luxurious kind. Oh, that's cool, I thought at the time. I might be able to use that someday.

Just around the time of that visit to Rich, we had been asking our customers—Walmart and Home Depot and the others—for ideas as to what they would like to see TerraCycle make next.

Soon after the lawsuit settled, we were at Home Depot

pitching our products for the next selling season. The meeting was going well, and when we were almost done, I said to the buyer, "I'm sure I can find a way to make anything out of garbage, at a better price than anyone else can make it from new materials. What are you looking for?" The buyer said that he felt there was a gap in the composter product line. The company wanted a home composter that could retail at a strong price (under $200) and be more appealing than the plastic composters that had dominated the market.

Composters range from ultra-low-tech—basically a holder for a pile of kitchen and garden wastes—to very complicated containers with multiple compartments that sort of automate the mixing of the materials until they become compost. Basically, all a composter needs to do is hold organic waste material as it breaks down. It needs an opening, ideally with a door that can close securely, where you can put in the waste and take out the compost. You can speed up the process by mixing up the materials, so being able to rotate the container is also a good feature. Also, since it will likely be kept outdoors, it should be watertight and strong enough to keep out raccoons and other critters.

Robin and Bill and I were tossing ideas back and forth, and I remembered the wine barrels. Robin agreed that they were perfect, and we sat down and designed it that day; ending up with a very simple design: turn the barrel on its side, cut a hole in the end, attach a door to it, and the barrel instantly becomes a rotary composter. You could roll it with your foot. Later that day we added a simple base with four casters. We set the barrel on the casters and, voilà, it rotated easily. The next day I was in Atlanta showing it to the Home Depot buyer, who loved it and agreed to test it in a large number of stores. "Oh, and by the way," the buyer said, "we're also looking for a good rain barrel—again, competitive price and better looking than the plastic ones. Lots of parts of the country are experiencing drought, and people are more interested in collecting rain to water the garden. See what you can do with that."

We could do a lot with it. A wine barrel would be ideal for collecting rain, since it has the essential feature of being watertight, can hold fifty-five gallons of liquid, is beautiful to look at, has a great story, and even smells of Napa Valley wine. All you have to do is cut a hole in the top and attach two spigots, and suddenly you have a rain barrel that is much more attractive than any plastic barrel but retails at close to the same price.

All we had to do was figure out how to manufacture the composters and rain barrels. At least this time, we figured, we knew where the barrels would come from, but we didn't really have anybody to do the carpentry in Trenton. We didn't want to invest a lot of money in setting up a production site, since there was always the possibility that the composter wouldn't work in the test marketing. In other words, it was the usual TerraCycle product development cycle.

Why Can't Everything Be Made from Waste?

We looked everywhere for a carpenter, but they didn't seem to be common in Trenton. In the middle of the search, I had to go to New York for an event for HP computers. HP was doing a commercial that featured us—profiling Terra-Cycle as a small company that used HP computers for its business operations. The company sent down a limo to Trenton to pick me up and take me to New York, and during the whole ride I was on the phone with Robin, talking about how hard it was to find a good carpenter. At the end of the trip, the driver turned around and said, in a thick Hispanic accent, "Excuse me, sir, I know I should not have been listening to your conversation . . . but, sir, I would like to be your carpenter."

I couldn't believe it. He said that he was from Costa Rica originally and had worked as a carpenter there. When he decided to move to the United States with his family, he couldn't find any work but driving limos. I told him to come to the office and we'd talk it over.

Ron, the driver, showed up the next day and got the job.

Meanwhile, Robin had been talking to our investor who owned the winery. It turned out that he didn't turn over nearly enough barrels every year to supply us. Ironically, we had gained a carpenter and lost the wine barrels. So Robin started calling all the larger wineries, which would have a higher turnover of barrels. Since the schedule for used wine barrels is dependent on when winemakers feel that their wine is ready, as sources we found them spotty and entirely inconsistent. However, the barrels were cheap: a barrel that the winemaker had paid about $1,000 for, and used only one time, cost us $15 including transportation.

We brought our first small shipment of barrels to Trenton, just enough to fill the test market order for Home Depot, and put Ron to work. Everything went fine—Ron did good work and we fulfilled the order on time. The product blew off the shelves, and of course that meant we would have to do the same thing again, but in a much greater volume. There wasn't really enough space in the Trenton factory to do the work of converting a large number of barrels, and, besides, we didn't really want to ship the barrels from California to Trenton and then ship them back, in some cases, to customers in California. It was obvious that the construction should be done in California, which meant that we would have to go there and find somewhere to do it. As always, time was running out.

I flew out to California to look for a production site. The thing about barrels, after all, is that they're big. They're about five feet tall and four feet in diameter at the widest, so you need a lot of warehouse space to deal with them. The issue very quickly became where to put all the barrels. The people at one of the vineyards we were getting barrels from asked where we would want all of the barrels shipped to.

"Well, I'll have to get back to you about that," I said. "I'm actually here looking for a place to convert the barrels." We really just needed a big open space where our carpenter could do the necessary work.

"We've got a big old barn in the back that we're not using," they said. "Would that be the kind of thing you need?" I was so relieved that I took a quick look at the barn and told them that we'd take it.

But now I had to tell Ron that the operation was moving twenty-five hundred miles west. I flew back to Trenton, trying to figure out how to put it to him. I felt really bad that we had basically offered him a job and now were taking it away from him. When I got to work, I called him into my office and said, "Look, Ron, we're very happy with your work, but we've realized that we just won't be able to make the composters and rain barrels here in Trenton. There just isn't space."

He didn't bat an eye. "Okay," he said. "Where do you want me to go?"

I hadn't expected this. "Well, we have this space in California. . . ."

"Okay," he said. "When do you want me to be there?"

The next day, he packed his family and belongings into a car and drove to California.

As usual, we were under the gun. We had to get that order ready in a hurry. There were a lot of shipments of different sizes going to different places, and the forms from the big retailers are always complicated, so Robin flew out a week before the shipment had to be ready to troubleshoot any difficulties. He called up after he'd been there for a while.

"Tom, did you look at this barn before you leased it?"

Uh-oh, I thought. "Of course I did. I didn't inspect every inch of it. It was just what we needed, where we needed it, and it was available. Is there something wrong?"

"You could say that. It doesn't have any electricity, for one thing. Ron needs electricity to cut the barrels."

"Well, you can rent a generator, right?"

"It doesn't have a bathroom, either."

"You're on a farm in the middle of nowhere; I'm sure as a man you could improvise."

"It doesn't have a floor. There's just dirt."

"Well, yes, but you don't really need a concrete floor for the barrels."

"Tom, the roof leaks. And it's been raining for three days."

Robin finished the order literally up to his knees in muck. He got the order out, on time, and Home Depot had a terrific success with them. The rain barrels especially. They couldn't keep them in the stores. Once again, we had satisfied a need with garbage.

Just as with our first sale to Walmart, the successful upcycling of wine barrels into composters and rain barrels had a momentum of its own. Now we were known not only as an organic plant food company but as a company that had a much broader range of products. We had created distinctive products from garbage, and other companies began coming to us, asking us to create something for them. Target came to us and asked us to make a clock out of garbage. We started looking at vinyl records and realized that if you heat them just a bit, you can mold them into any shape you want.

We slowly came up with a theory on how to solve all waste. The first step is to look at any object as made from three components: the material it is made from, the form it is in, and its intended purpose. Then, when viewing waste along these three distinct aspects, solving it becomes much more manageable. We thought at that time, and have now found, that every consumer waste stream, from cigarette butts to dirty diapers to used chewing gum, can be either reused (values the material, form, and intention), upcycled (values the material and form), or recycled (values the material). No exceptions have been found so far.

The only thing better than having waste solutions is to not produce or use anything, since the less that is produced the less that becomes waste. In other words, if we all stopped buying stuff, then many of our environmental problems would be alleviated as the strain on our resources would be diminished.

Coming to this realization was a journey. A year after we first began using the wine barrels in our production, we decided to use the other part of the wine waste stream: in an effort to make a corkboard for OfficeMax we created the first mass-produced used-wine-cork corkboard.

My view of waste had completely changed. I was walking around and every time I saw something that we typically consider waste I was looking at it as a commodity, an object, and trying to analyze what valuable features that object had that could be used to make a product.

Over time I started to discover another element of waste that could lead to another way to classify it. This has to do with how much people care about the waste that is being produced. For example, every business produces office waste. Because every business produces these forms of waste, generally, employees and by extension the businesses themselves feel relatively little ownership of, or responsibility for, that waste. Another category of business waste is industry-specific waste, such as plastic foam packaging for electronics. Businesses and employees seem to care about these kinds of waste only if everyone in the industry starts to care.

But there is another kind of waste, such as all those candy bar wrappers and plastic juice cartons and toothpaste tubes. They have a very unique characteristic: they all have a company's brand on them. Think about a product—Stonyfield yogurt. Yogurt containers are made of a certain kind of plastic that is not recyclable in today's national recycling infrastructure. So a container of Stonyfield is bought, the contents are eaten, and the package is thrown out. Until the moment that the consumer (who owns the container) throws it out, it serves as an advertisement for Stonyfield Farm. If the container winds up as a piece of litter crushed on the sidewalk, it will serve as a negative advertisement, affecting the brand image the company invested millions of dollars to build. Stonyfield Farm, like many companies, would pay to avoid negative advertising.

I call this waste stream "branded waste." Companies care about it more than any other waste form, since it has their name plastered on it. The full realization came to fruition when I got a call from my friend Seth Goldman, the cofounder and TeaEO of Honest Tea.

CHAPTER 10

Branded Waste and the Launch of Sponsored Waste

I first met Seth Goldman at an *Inc.* maga-zine panel about encouraging entrepreneurship, but we didn't start talking about juice pouches until a later conference on organic products. Seth makes tea. He launched Honest Tea in 1998 out of his kitchen, and it's now the best-selling bottled tea in the natural foods industry. In 2011, Honest Tea was sold to Coca-Cola for a healthy sum. The name, by the way, came from his partner, Barry Nalebuff. Barry had just returned from India, where he had been analyzing the tea industry for a case study. Among other things, Barry had learned that most of the tea leaves purchased for brewing and bottling by American companies was the lower-quality residue left after the higher-quality tea leaves had been separated out. Barry had even come up with a name to describe a bottled tea that was made with real tea leaves—Honest Tea. Seth agreed that it was the perfect name to fit an all-natural brand that would "strive to create healthy and honest relationships with its customers, suppliers and the environment," as the company's Web site puts it. Five weeks later, he took some of the tea drinks he'd made to Whole Foods and found himself with an order for fifteen thousand bottles. Even though he didn't have a factory. Sounded very familiar to me.

At the organic products conference, Seth brought up a problem that had just come up in his business. He had spent months getting ready to launch Honest Kids, a line of juice drinks for kids that, like Honest's adult drinks, would contain less sugar and no artificial ingredients—a pure organic juice drink for children. However, whereas drinks marketed for adults were sold in recyclable glass and plastic bottles, juice pouches were the only way to really compete for the kid market. Juice pouches are big items for kids—more than 5 billion of them are sold each year in the United States alone.

And unfortunately all of them end up in landfills. Juice pouches fuse plastic with aluminum into a single material, which renders them nonrecyclable. With that said, they are preferred as a packaging form as they are much lighter and convenient for kids on the go.

Branded Waste and the Launch of Sponsored Waste

This was Seth's problem. His healthier juice-pouch drink was about to be packaged in what William McDonough and Michael Braungart call a "monstrous hybrid" in their book *Cradle to Cradle*. They point out that we have compounded the difficulties of recycling by putting together materials that, individually, might degrade naturally or be recycled—but in combination are totally resistant to either. While aluminum by itself can be recycled easily, and some plastics can be recycled (specifically, the plastic in Seth's juice pouches), when you put the two together, there's nothing you can do but throw it into a landfill. So he asked me if we could come up with a solution to keep all of those used juice pouches from heading for that fate. I realized during that call from Seth that for the first time someone was asking us to solve brand-specific waste. What concerned him was that Honest Kids juice pouches would wind up being litter. Mangled and dirty.

In other words, companies like Seth's would potentially invest money to solve a branded waste problem.

This is the challenge that all nonrecyclable waste faces—from a Starbucks paper coffee cup to a Bimbo plastic bread bag to the waxed box or flexible plastic that holds your frozen vegetables and ice cream.

Not long after I started talking to Seth, I got a call from

Gary Hirshberg, the CE-Yo of Stonyfield Farm yogurt, asking me to create a similar solution for his yogurt cups. It felt like the universe was trying to tell me something.

Naturally, I was happy to try to find solutions for Seth and Gary. Starting with the drink pouch, we first tried to figure out how a pouch could be manipulated to make it useful in a different way. What are the characteristics of a pouch that make it useful? Well, it's quite strong, and it's about three by five inches in size. The only challenge is how to attach them together to create a fabric in a simple way. That reminded me of something I had heard at a conference I'd attended about a group of Filipino women.

130

PREDA—People's Recovery, Empowerment and Development Assistance—was founded in 1974 in the Philippines by Father Shay Cullen, an Irish Colombian missionary, and Merle and Alex Hermoso, a Filipino couple dedicated to helping Filipino youth. The foundation's original goal was to help teenagers from broken homes who were trying to forget their problems through substance abuse, to help the children "deal with their family problems and to rehabilitate the parents and restore family unity, respect and love." To do that, PREDA tried to find ways for its people to earn a living.

Beginning in September 2004, PREDA began producing, selling, and shipping items made from juice pouches, which are just as common in the Philippines as in this country. They train those who collect the used juice bags (including many students, who help their schools earn money by collecting juice bags on campus), paying them for their efforts and teaching them about the environment. After the collected containers are cleaned and sanitized, PREDA makes them available to the group's women (and men), who use them to produce handcrafted items. As of April 2006, PREDA had sold more than 46,500 bags worldwide. So juice pouches could be upcycled into a material—maybe not what you would call fabric, but something that could be sewn into sheets and cut or folded or sewn into any shape you needed.

This seemed to be a perfect model for TerraCycle to use in solving Seth's problem. As usual, none of this occurred to me until a few days before we were supposed to meet with Seth in his Bethesda office and present the idea to him. So we went to Target and bought a couple hundred Honest Kids juice pouches and brought them back to the office. Everybody drank Honest Kids for a couple of days until we had enough pouches to wash and experiment with.

We were supposed to meet Seth the next day, June 27, 2007. So I bought a sewing machine at Walmart and spent all night with it, first learning how to sew—the biggest problem was threading the machine and breaking needles. Once I had mastered that, I had to figure out how to put together pouches. If you look at a picture of an Honest Kids pouch, you'll see that it's curved in the middle—where people can grip it. So I had to figure out how to sew the curves of the pouch together. Not to mention designing what the finished product would look like. Sometime after midnight I had the first Honest Kids drink-pouch tote bag.

Not many hours later, I got up to drive to Maryland for our meeting with Seth. Seth loved the idea, loved the bag, and immediately bought into the whole sponsored waste program; more important, he offered to pay for it. With his investment, we could open up six hundred locations to collect the pouches.

There is something miraculous about that moment to me. With one simple handshake (and a financial commitment), Honest Kids drink pouches stopped having only one fate—being garbage; three years later we were actively collecting more drink pouches via our brigade than Honest Tea was making! Suddenly those drink pouches were not just garbage; they had value (two cents each). Seth's investment, made in order to prevent his pouches from becoming garbage, had made his pouches valuable—to TerraCycle and to the schools and other organizations that would collect them.

Of course we couldn't start with all six hundred locations, but we prepared to set up one hundred of them around the country as a test. We offered them up on the Web site, and within twenty-four hours, we had filled the list. We had to close the offer temporarily and put names on a waiting list.

Branded Waste and the Launch of Sponsored Waste

Almost the same thing happened with the yogurt cups. When you look at an object in a waste stream, you want to try to use it for the value it already has. The key to rethinking garbage is to use as little energy as possible—a lot of energy has been spent to shape the plastic into a yogurt cup, so the best outcome is if we do as little as possible to change that. The idea that came to us was to reuse the yogurt cups as planting pots, which also fit nicely into our established selling lines to Home Depot and other home improvement stores and departments. Gardeners toss about 320 million pounds of plastic every year, and plant pots are a significant part of that total. We showed it to Gary, who loved the idea. Gary joined in to sponsor a yogurt brigade a couple of weeks after we'd launched Seth's drink-pouch one. The yogurt brigade, like the drink-pouch brigade, was a huge success, which just drove home the fact that there was a tremendous demand to solve the problem of waste—bigger even than I had imagined.

As the drink-pouch brigade was gearing up, I started pitching this new material concept to retailers, and the response was even more enthusiastic than I ever expected. Walgreens, Target, Shopko, Walmart, OfficeMax, Meijer, and a few others all agreed to carry various juice-pouch products— we were ready to go with pencil cases, tote bags, backpacks, homework folders, lunch boxes, and other products. The retailers loved them. They were great, unique products with that Andy Warhol kind of look, but just as important to them was the story of the product. We were offering something that was environmentally better than anything currently on the market, and the raw material (the juice pouches) had been collected most likely by a child in a school or a member of a church or a charity somewhere in America. And those organizations had received two cents per pouch as a donation. As you can imagine, they couldn't get enough. After articles in *NEA Today* and *Guideposts* in April 2007, the number of locations collecting bottles shot up from fifteen hundred to four thousand in just a few months. The Honest Tea juice-pouch brigade and the Stonyfield Farm yogurt brigade were also receiving an enormous amount of publicity.

134

After a sales meeting with one of America's biggest retailers, I called up Robin and said, "The good news is that Walgreens just gave us a huge new order for the juice-pouch pencil cases."

"Fabulous. But what's the bad news?"

"Well, I've done a rough calculation on how many juice pouches we'll need to make the order."

"Yeah, and . . . ?"

"I figure it will be about ten million juice pouches. And we'll need to start manufacturing in about two weeks."

The big problem was that there weren't enough drink pouches coming in from the brigade. That wasn't a surprise; we knew the brigade would build slowly, as it's very much a word-of-mouth program. But we also hadn't expected the size of the response from the retailers. Robin went on the Internet, and after an all-night search he found a company called Encorp in Vancouver. It was actually an arm of the government of British Columbia, which had mandated that juice pouches in schools have a deposit on them, sort of like a bottle bill in the United States. This meant that lots of people were collecting them in BC to get back the deposit (which shows what a little economic incentive can do). They had started the Canadian equivalent of a juice-pouch brigade, but the catch was that they didn't have a good solution for processing them. They couldn't be dumped in a landfill, so until they found a solution, they had to warehouse them.

But "warehouse" isn't the right word, because what they'd done was to put the juice pouches through a baler, which just squashes them into a highly compressed cube. So they wound up with hundreds of three-by-three-by-three-foot blocks of juice pouches, each of which weighed maybe a half ton. They didn't wash them, they didn't take out the straws, they didn't even take them out of the plastic bags they were collected in. Then, since there wasn't anybody who could recycle them, the juice-pouch cubes were being stored in trailers parked in a field in British Columbia. And this had been going on for a couple of years.

So Robin called up someone at Encorp and asked, "Do you have any juice pouches?"

He kind of chuckled and said, "Yeah."

"Well, do you have any idea how many you might have?"

"Oh, I'd say . . . I guess about twenty million."

That was the right number. Robin was beginning to get excited. "Can I have them?"

"I don't know if I can give them to you." Oh, yeah, Robin thought, it's the government. "I'll have to talk to people here. Why don't you send us some information about your company so that we can talk it over here?"

It took Robin about a split second to shoot off a letter about TerraCycle and the unique way we upcycle waste, and how we would use the pouches to make great pencil cases and backpacks and lots of other things for kids. No response. Robin waited a day and called again. Somebody important was on holiday. He'd be back in three weeks. Robin found someone else to talk to and emphasized that we really needed the pouches, and if we didn't get them soon, we would have to go somewhere else.

Finally one guy said, "We're thinking about it."

That was enough for Robin. He bought an airline ticket and flew to Vancouver to meet with the Encorp official. We needed to see the pouches firsthand to know whether we could use them. The first thing Robin did, then, was ask to see the bales. So someone went to a trailer with a forklift—in the pouring rain, typical BC weather—and hauled over a hunk of massed juice pouches that was drenched and leaking. It stunk due to the juice having fermented there for months or potentially years. The Encorp guy looked at Robin as if to say, "There's no way in the world you want this stuff, is there?" He bent down to the dripping square block of juice pouches in front of Robin and yanked on one of the plastic bag handles until about twenty or thirty pouches came flying out. After looking at them closely and realizing there was no other choice, Robin asked if he could get them all.

Everything was falling into place until Encorp brought up the last, and biggest, problem. Almost all the drink pouches—both from the brigade and the ones that Encorp had collected—were Capri Sun and Kool-Aid brand. Both of those brands are owned by Kraft Foods, the biggest food company in America. The Encorp people would not release the pouches to us unless they had assurance that Kraft was on board with TerraCycle reusing its pouches. Since we had just resolved the lawsuit with Scotts Miracle-Gro, and years before had had to get licenses from Coke and Pepsi, we decided we had only one choice.

I called Kraft.

CHAPTER **11**

Sponsored Waste Takes Off

Would a corporate giant like Kraft be willing to have its logo on a TerraCycle pencil case or backpack? I had no idea.

What I did know was that if Kraft was going to oppose the project, I had a serious problem on my hands, as Encorp wouldn't allow us to bring down the juice boxes it had been stockpiling.

The question of intellectual property rights concerning waste is tricky. Obviously, all these brands have various levels of intellectual property protection. For example, no one can come along and use the built-up power of the brand name, its attributes, or its look—in other words, its trade dress—to sell

139

one's own product. But the laws, and the interpretations of the laws, are still very vague when it comes to waste. It's possible that Capri Sun doesn't own the shape and design of its juice pouch if the pouch is sewn together with pouches from other brands of juice and made into a tote bag.

The first surprise was that Kraft had a vice president in charge of "sustainability." He directed me to Vinay, who was the brand manager for Capri Sun. I sent him an e-mail explaining that TerraCycle manufactures eco-friendly, affordable products that are made from and packaged in waste. I gave him some examples and described the brigades and how people (of all ages) were involved with the programs and how educational it could be for them.

All I told him about the juice pouches was that we were in the midst of launching a line of pencil cases and tote bags made from various sewn-together drink pouches to be sold by major retailers the following spring, and that the idea had already generated the promise of very good publicity in several major magazines. I said I'd like to meet with him to describe the program in more detail. Luckily, *20/20* was going to broadcast a feature on TerraCycle that very Friday.

Within a day or so, he responded:

Thanks for reaching out to me. Would love to meet up in person. I have read about TerraCycle and am very intrigued by what you guys do. In addition to the new line of bags and pencil cases, I'd love to talk to you about the pouch brigade and how (or if) we can get involved. Environmental consciousness is becoming top of mind for even the younger consumers today, and Capri Sun needs to be part of the trend.

Early in November 2007, Albe and I went up to see Vinay for the first time in his office in Tarrytown, New York.

You couldn't find a place more different from TerraCycle's Trenton factory than Kraft's Tarrytown offices. "One day TerraCycle will have a campus like this," I told Albe.

Needless to say, we were completely out of place. Even the receptionist who handed us our visitor's passes looked at us funny. We were dressed pretty much as usual, in jeans and T-shirts, and of course we were carrying tote bags and backpacks and pencil cases that we'd made up with Capri Sun juice pouches (maybe it was the backpacks that caught her eye).

When we got to Vinay's office, he couldn't have been more welcoming. The first thing he said to us was, "Okay, we're in. How shall we make this work?" I quickly saw not only that we would be able to work out a licensing agreement that would allow TerraCycle to use the Capri Sun and Kool-Aid pouches but that he was expecting to talk about becoming a sponsor.

In that brief conversation we had taken a huge step forward. We walked out of the meeting with a licensing agreement and a handshake on a plan to work together on a sponsorship agreement.

On February 6, 2008, we signed a contract that would scale up the drink-pouch brigade from the six hundred locations we had at the time to five thousand.

Honest Kids represented perhaps one-tenth of 1 percent of the drink-pouch market in the United States. Capri Sun and Kool-Aid together represented well over 90 percent. Almost 80 percent of all juice pouches are consumed in schools, so pouches are ideal not only from the standpoint of the school raising funds but also in terms of the educational value of upcycling versus trashing the pouch. By working out this agreement with Capri Sun we were able to create a program that essentially locked up the entire drink-pouch market, created a scalable national upcycling infrastructure, and could create real, massive change. No longer would more than 5 billion drink pouches wind up in landfills every year. Over the first five years of the program the collections per month scaled up from fifteen hundred drink pouches per month in the first year to 10 million pouches per month five years later.

All this was exactly what large companies like Kraft were looking for. The concern about climate change that was put in sharp focus by Al Gore's book *An Inconvenient Truth* was beginning to affect all large corporations. Kraft was not unusual in having formed a sustainability division. What the companies were discovering was that being environmentally conscious could reduce their costs and increase their profitability.

Capri Sun's support was just the tip of the iceberg. Now that we had a program with that brand, other Kraft brands started showing interest. We started getting calls from Oreo, Chips Ahoy!, and Balance Bar to see if we could help them out.

While we were launching the program with Kraft, we were approached by Clif Bar, a company founded by Gary Erickson—he has a story that is a lot like Seth's. A serious cyclist and also the owner of a bakery in Berkeley, California, he didn't like any of the energy bars that were available. So in 1992, he started making his own energy bar—the Clif Bar, named after his father—and his enterprise quickly became one of the fastest-growing companies in the United States. In 2000, Gary turned down a $120 million offer for the company. Just as it is for Honest Tea, environmental awareness is a key principle in his business, and Clif Bar came to us to see if we could upcycle Clif Bar wrappers. Since these wrappers are hybrids—part aluminum, like juice pouches—they are also not recyclable and a fantastic candidate for upcycling. Within a month, the Clif Bar energy bar wrapper brigade was launched.

143

Revolution in a Bottle

Like the juice pouches, Oreo and Chips Ahoy! cookie package wrappers and Clif Bar wrappers are not recyclable, but for a different reason. They are composed of several superthin layers of different kinds of plastics, each of which provides a different advantage in terms of protecting the cookies from moisture, air, and sunlight; keeping them fresh whenever you open that package; and making it easy to print nice graphics on them.

A lighter wrapper is "environmentally beneficial because it uses less material and less energy per package," says David Cornell, technical director of the Association of Postconsumer Plastic Recyclers in Washington, D.C. "This is all fine and dandy until the package gets to the end of its life." What we knew was that the end of its life as a package was only the beginning of its life as a pencil pouch or the like. The brand managers were extremely excited to see what we could do for them, and several of them immediately began work launching brigades. Within a couple of months, we had launched the cookie wrapper brigade with sponsorship from Oreo, Chips Ahoy! and Nabisco (the three largest cookie brands in America). Balance Bar and South Beach Diet Bar became sponsors alongside Clif Bar on the energy bar wrapper brigade.

This landslide embracement at Kraft was exactly the opposite of what I thought would happen, but it was an indication of just how enormous the potential of sponsored waste was. Kraft is the biggest food company in America, with more than $30 billion in sales per year. Different flavors of Oreos and Chips Ahoy! are the four largest-selling cookie brands in America and sell hundreds of millions of packages per year. Our partnership with Kraft took the little idea that we had pioneered with Honest Tea, Stonyfield Farm, and Clif Bar and expanded it to megascale.

There is an irony in this. Gary Hirshberg came up with the idea of Stonyfield Farm because he took a tour of a Kraft-sponsored pavilion on the future of food at Disney World's Epcot Center in Florida. At the time he was head of a non-profit organization called the New Alchemy Institute, which studied how to produce food and energy with no fossil fuels. In 1982 (the year I was born), he went to visit his mother, who was then the senior buyer at Epcot. He happened to visit when Kraft was running a pavilion that offered its view of how foods would be produced in the future, and he found the ideas shocking. "But the big shocker of that day was not the incredible widespread use of fossil fuels and CO_2 emissions and so on, it was the fact that, for the twenty-five thousand people who visited my institute every year, that many people visited them every day." He realized that if he was going to have a real impact on the environment, he would have to be as big as Kraft.

As you look at any waste material, like wrappers, you need to focus on what basic materials you can make from it and what form they are in. Reuse is not an option for a wrapper like it is for a yogurt cup, but you can upcycle and recycle it. For example, Oreo wrappers can be upcycled by fusing them into a sewable fabric from which one can make everything from bags to shower curtains. They can also be recycled by melting them into an injection moldable plastic that can be made into anything from trash cans and cups . . . fundamentally anything. And that's just the beginning. To put it into perspective, all of these TerraCycle products were in widespread big-box distribution before the end of 2008 (almost one year from the date the cookie wrapper brigade was launched).

Perhaps the biggest benefit of all is that the TerraCycle system of collecting and solving waste allows a brand to make products that are "not recyclable" "recyclable." By 2012 that exact TerraCycle message appeared on 40 billion packages per year around the world.

The brands started taking notice of the marketing value of this proposition. Capri Sun launched a thirty-second commercial on Cartoon Network in late 2008, highlighting the drink-pouch brigade and the products that TerraCycle makes from the pouches. From full-page advertisements in national magazines to advertising on the Web, the marketing of these programs by Kraft allowed a new "megascale" to be realized. To me the biggest win of all was that in late 2008 each Chips Ahoy! package and all Capri Sun boxes started carrying a description of the TerraCycle program—more than a half billion packages highlighting the TerraCycle solution, as recycling is highlighted on bottles.

On July 1, 2008, we officially launched the program in the media with a leadoff article in the *Wall Street Journal* that began:

> Each year, billions of food and drink wrappers encasing popular brands end up in landfills because their multilayered materials—which keep products fresh—are tricky and expensive to break down and recycle. This waste has presented a challenge for manufacturers eager to reduce their environmental impact and buff reputations among eco-conscious consumers.
>
> But that's changing due to an unusual alliance between a growing number of food and beverage bigwigs—including Kraft Foods Inc., Kellogg Co., Clif Bar & Co. and Coca-Cola Co.—and a tiny company in Trenton, N.J., named TerraCycle Inc.
>
> "What TerraCycle has done so well is they've created products that aren't boring," says Ryan Vero, chief merchandising officer at OfficeMax, which stocks TerraCycle's Capri Sun and Kool-Aid

binders and pencil pouches and has ordered computer bags for the fall. "That's cool for back to
school. We even have executives carrying them
around this building."

Shortly after we announced our partnership with Kraft
we got calls from Frito-Lay, Mars, 3M, GlaxoSmithKline,
Nestlé, and many other companies about launching similar
national brigade programs.

By 2012 more than 30 million people were collecting millions of pieces of waste with TerraCycle every day. Everything
from juice pouches to used chewing gum to asthma inhalers.
The impact on the environment is significant. Not only are
we keeping major volumes of nonrecyclable materials from
ending up in landfills, we are eliminating the need for that
same quantity of new nonrecyclable materials from ever
being produced. You can even return the products we make
via the brigades when you are done with them.

CHAPTER 12

Upcycled Marketing

Just as the sponsored waste programs
were gearing up, I was asked to give a keynote address to
Target's executive team, during that company's design week.
Afterward, a few of the Target folks took me out to dinner,
and at one point I turned to a Target marketing executive and
asked, "Sally, what waste problem can we solve for you?" She
laughed and said, "Plastic bags. You can solve our plastic bag
problem." The reason she laughed is because plastic bags are
so common, so universal, and such an enormous environmental problem that it seemed inconceivable to her that anyone could really do very much about it.

149

Revolution in a Bottle

It's difficult, in fact, to get a handle on how many plastic bags there are in the world, or what happens to them. It's also amazing how recently they have become a problem. The basic plastic shopping bag was only created in the late 1970s by a man named Gordon Dancy. (Before his death, he began a business dedicated to recycling plastic.) Thirty years later, the world uses somewhere around 1 trillion bags each year (the number is hard to pin down precisely). The United States alone uses nearly 400 billion bags and wraps of all kinds every year. That's more than a thousand bags per year for every man, woman, and child in the country. According to the *Wall Street Journal*, Americans use 100 billion plastic shopping bags alone yearly, which consumes 12 million barrels of oil and costs retailers $4 billion—the cost of which, of course, is passed on to us, the consumers.

Estimates vary, but most say that the percentage of plastic bags that are recycled is in the single digits. But the worst part is that plastic bags can't be broken down by biological processes, which is the fastest way to break down something without creating pollutants. Light is the main way that plastic bags degrade, and it works very slowly. So they blow around our streets and rivers and oceans for years and years. They are eaten by sea turtles, who mistake them for jellyfish. And even when they start to degrade, they still don't disappear. They just break up into smaller and smaller bits over a period as long as one thousand years. These bits, which are great at soaking up some kinds of toxic chemicals, are ingested by fish—and therefore probably by us.

The situation is so serious that governments are getting into the act. In 2002 Ireland instituted an extremely successful plastic bag consumption tax, PlasTax. Consumers paid an extra fifteen cents per bag that they took from the store. Not only did the tax reduce consumption by 90 percent, it also brought in almost $10 million, which was used to set up a fund for environmental projects.

But it seems unlikely that more taxes will make much headway in the United States anytime soon, and local bans will remain just that, local. Ireland became a success story because its people enthusiastically accepted the idea—it became a social black mark to be seen carrying a disposable plastic bag.

So that was the challenge from Target—although really it was more of a joking aside, in Sally's mind.

Later on, I looked around on the Internet and, lo and behold, there were instructions on how to solve the problem. Do it yourself and see—just search on "fuse plastic bags." At a site called Etsy.com, where participants are dedicated to making things by hand and telling people how to make things by hand, I saw a video on how to fuse plastic bags with an ordinary household iron. You flatten out the bags, put them between some wax paper so the plastic doesn't melt onto your iron, and heat them about fifteen seconds on each side.

In the end you wind up with a durable material that you can use to make all sorts of things, just like the material we created from juice pouches but lighter and more flexible.

So naturally I got an iron—this time from Target—and collected some plastic bags and took them into the Terra-Cycle office. Albe and I played around with a tote bag design for a while, and then I asked Pierre, who had also worked on our brigades with Honest Tea and Stonyfield, to take over the project. Pierre came to TerraCycle from Seattle, and he had flown three thousand miles to interview for a job we posted on Craigslist.

The ironing process isn't really hard to do, but there is a learning curve, and in Pierre's case the cost of the learning curve was paid by our conference table, which to this day has burnt plastic bag residue on it. We tried different thicknesses of plastic bags and wound up with eight layers for the bottom of our tote bag and two layers on the sides. We had solved Sally's problem, in about a week.

The last part of the development was to figure out how to mass-produce the fusing process. We clearly couldn't just buy a lot of irons and do it ourselves. Eventually we were able to construct a machine that looks a little like the pants presser that dry cleaners use. Soon we had a sewn tote bag made from twenty-five plastic shopping bags in mass.

Sally was astonished and delighted. Soon afterward, Target put in a huge order for what was later christened a "reTote." They began to ship us the bags they had been collecting from their California stores (where, by law, stores that carry groceries, including Target, must collect them). This consisted of a truckload of bags a week (roughly a quarter of a million bags in each truck). By this time, we had simply run out of space in the Trenton factory. We were making so many products—probably thirty at that point. It was clear to me that we would be making many more soon. So we found a huge empty space in another part of Trenton—nearly a block long, 250,000 square feet.

Just about this time, still early in 2008, *Newsweek* invited me to a meeting to decide on the content for its Earth Day issue. The magazine had invited a lot of people in the environmental world, from both nonprofits and business. Seth Goldman and Gary Hirshberg were there, for instance.

Even magazines have a waste problem, although the technology has improved a great deal in recent years, so that although glossy magazines are recycled more often, it's still rare that the cover of a glossy magazine, with its heavy inks, is recycled.

What if the cover of the magazine itself could become a shipping envelope? The outside, of course, would be editorial—a big photo and headlines. But the inside could have a shipping label printed on it with our address. I picked up a napkin and doodled about how someone could detach the magazine cover, refold it, and tape three sides to make an envelope. Then the person could fill it with whatever he or she wanted to send to TerraCycle, tape it closed, and put it in the mailbox. Instantly, the magazine cover becomes a recycling bin with paid postage.

I was in Minnesota a couple of days later, talking to Target. I saw Sally in one of the halls and asked her if Target would be interested, and she said instantly, "We're in." Target ultimately bought the entire cover and did the promotion three times after *Newsweek*, including once in *People* magazine.

After Target said yes, we did some testing and wound up figuring that it would take a person about two hours to actually do the entire promotion. That is, the person would have to remove the cover, do the mechanics of making the envelope, find some bags to put in it, and take it to the post office. Based on that, we somehow estimated that we would receive maybe five thousand "cover envelopes" back.

It was a thrill to pick up that copy of *Newsweek*, just months after we were given the plastic bag challenge by Sally.

The first week, we received three thousand bags, well beyond our expectations, but that was nothing compared to what came the next week. Thank God the post office accepted these folded magazine covers in the mail! We inundated the Trenton post office. By the fourth week, we had received more than forty thousand magazine covers—they sent us trucks filled with them. The amazing thing was that 99.9

percent of the bags we received were Target bags. We had to bring in people and train them about how to fuse the bags—and which ones to use. Folks had left all kinds of things in the bags—receipts, coins, chewing gum, and some things that I don't even want to mention. We had sixty people in Trenton fusing twenty-four/seven, three shifts. Since each reTote was composed of twenty-five plastic bags, that opening order alone saved just over 800,000 plastic bags.

Then Target sent all the participants a coupon for a reTote. Amazingly coupon redemption was over 60 percent (typically anything over 1 percent is deemed a success). People, when surveyed, said it was because they felt like they had made the product. Which in fact they had.

The reTote opened our eyes to the endless marketing possibilities of our new sponsored waste system. The major challenge of sustainability inside for-profit entities is that while they do care about sustainability, their corporate social responsibility officers can command major funding only if they can show relatively short-term return on investment for their actions. For example, spending millions of dollars on offsetting a company's carbon every year is very difficult to justify; the "investment" does not drive additional product sales when compared to putting funds into something like TV advertising.

Thus, as we evolved our sponsored waste programs, we realized we needed not only to help brands deal with the environmental impact of their postconsumer waste, but also to help our clients get measurable sales benefits from sponsoring our waste collection programs. We therefore put significant focus on how brands could leverage the marketing value of our services.

The core problem that the TerraCycle sponsored waste service solves is one of product end of life. If you are a company like Frito-Lay or Bic you have global packages and products (empty chip bags or spent pens) that are not recyclable in any country in the world. In other words, after their short lives they end up in either landfills or waste-to-energy facilities, creating an environmental negative. Before TerraCycle, all a manufacturer could do was to change its product and make it using recyclable materials. You could perhaps package your chips in a glass jar instead of a plastic bag. Consumers, however, want a certain price point and a certain convenience. Generally, this desire precludes brands from spending more money on recyclable packaging. In many cases, like a single-use pen, it isn't possible to construct the product in a way that would allow it to be recycled in local municipal recycling system.

Through sponsoring a TerraCycle national collection and solution program for a category of waste, a manufacturer (brand) immediately renders the waste nationally recyclable. By 2012 the TerraCycle message of recyclability (for example, "Recyclable through the TerraCycle network of collection programs" seen on Colgate packaging since 2011) was on more than 40 billion packages per year. TerraCycle can collect and recycle—through a private system—what municipal systems don't, because the economics of collection and solution are funded by the sponsor. Making the system worth the brand's while to pay, then, became the key to making the system work.

How do you show a brand that funding such a system is worth the money? The answer is short-term payback. Very quickly we established our strengths and the brands' strengths. On our end it was publicity, social media, and other media assets. On the brand end it was all paid media, from TV advertising to high-profile events.

We started seeing that brands, when they leveraged the fact that they were solving their waste, gained tremendous market share from their competitors that weren't—even though the collection programs are brand agnostic. For example, in Brazil in 2009, Tang (a powdered beverage mix like Crystal Light) generated about $500 million in sales. In 2010, Tang Brazil launched the TerraCycle program and dedicated much of its advertising focus on telling the story of how the pouches could be collected and recycled. The company deployed everything from commercials to billboards to communicate that consumers can help the environment when they keep Tang pouches out of landfills. The campaign not only lifted TerraCycle's visibility in Brazil but also increased

Tang's sales that year by 40 percent ($200 million) during a time when the entire beverages category declined by 2 percent nationally. The next year Tang launched the program in both Argentina and Mexico.

Now, the consumption of beverages didn't increase in Brazil because of our program; rather, consumers bought Tang instead of competing brands.

Soon brands all across the world were launching commercials and other marketing campaigns to promote their programs with TerraCycle. This ranged from L'Oréal running a major promotion in Times Square with a bunch of celebrities to show that cosmetic waste had a solution to Johnson & Johnson doing animated commercials in Europe talking about how its baby wipes packaging was now recyclable. The amazing thing is that not only are they promoting the new solution to their waste (for the first time taking active ownership of the problem) but they are also helping to grow the TerraCycle platform, using resources that are way beyond our company's means. It's a win-win situation.

One of the highlights of this newly found marketing strategy was a program that we conducted with Walmart USA in 2010. I met Andy at a conference where I was giving a keynote address in 2009. Andy is an imposing and modestly intimidating executive. Not only is he one of the leaders at Walmart but he offers you a handshake that I can still feel today.

Upcycled Marketing

Over a few months of discussions, Andy agreed to give TerraCycle forty feet of shelf space, six feet high, in all thirty-five hundred Walmart stores across the United States to highlight the brands that were sponsoring our brigade programs at the time (from Oreo to Capri Sun) and, beside them, to sell products that TerraCycle made from those brands' waste. This program resulted in close to $100 million of incremental sales for our brand partners and, ironically, almost cost me my job.

CHAPTER 13

The Art of Keeping One's Job

As TerraCycle's sales kept growing, our losses kept growing proportionally. In 2008 we hit $6.6 million in sales, but lost $4.5 million in the process. While our worm poop products were profitable, our new products, which made up a growing percentage of our total sales, were not. Since we were launching all sorts of sponsored waste programs we had to expand our product line constantly so that we could solve for the incoming waste. To make our products, we used a blend of outsourcing and in-house manufacturing, and because everything was made from waste we uncovered an array of unique headaches with each and every new product.

First it was hard to secure third-party manufacturers who would make the product at a prenegotiated price, or even when we did it was hard to keep them at that price once they understood the incremental challenges. This resulted in our scrambling to figure out how to scale up concepts and secure raw materials, technology, and partners to pull off big-box orders on a strict timeline and at breakneck prices. Daily problems ranged from how to press clockfaces into hundreds of thousands of used vinyl records for an order from Target (not to mention getting the records in the first place) to finding a partner to compress furniture shavings into fire starters for an order from Home Depot. When making everything from shower curtains to three-ring binders from waste, the problems are immense. My desire to do this in the Walmart world just compounded these challenges.

Sometime later that year I got a call from one of Terra-Cycle's board members asking me to have coffee with him one hour before a board meeting. During our sit-down he told me that the board, along with a few senior managers, had convened a few weeks before and decided that it was time for me to step aside and let a professional manager take over, one who could reverse the trend of our growing losses. In his hand he showed me a "360-degree management review" he had been working on during that month—little did I know it was a tool to have me replaced (it was sold to me as a "way to develop as a young leader").

Now, performance reviews are standard protocol in corporate America. The objective seems to be for the company to give formal and direct feedback to employees, who are assumed to understand that the reviews represent an opportunity to get a status check (like a report card) that can help them improve their performance and in the end further their careers.

I don't believe in formal performance reviews. I think they create an environment where employers risk not confronting unsatisfactory performance when it happens—or not acknowledging great work when it is delivered.

At TerraCycle, our approach has been to build a culture where feedback is given often and evenly to all employees. We do this through a reporting system that requires every department to submit a detailed biweekly report to the whole company (every employee). I greatly prefer this approach to a more formal, once-a-year sit-down. Someone who isn't performing well needs to know about it in real time, and someone who is doing great deserves immediate recognition.

Of course, this does leave one person who isn't part of the feedback loop. This is why our chairman suggested that I take part in a 360-degree evaluation that encourages employees to give anonymous feedback about a boss in a multi-rater system. But here's an important question: Is the role of a chief executive to be friendly and make everyone happy (which might result in positive 360-degree reviews)? Or is it to drive performance and return on investment for the owners or shareholders (which may produce more negative feedback)? I think most people would say it's the latter, and a strong chief may not be popular with the staff. Just look at Steve Jobs, a revolutionary who helped create the largest computer company in the world. He had a famously prickly, even tyrannical, personality. It's hard to imagine anyone persuading him to sit for a 360-degree review.

Of course, the irony is that while I thought I was driving shareholder value by growing revenue and increasing our product range I was also driving increasing losses every year.

While they were within their rights to ask for such a change, I was devastated. I clearly remember the moment sitting in that Jersey diner. After being told, the world slowed down. I got up out of the chrome diner booth, veins pulsating, pulling out two one-dollar bills for my coffee and placing them on the table. In a calm but stern voice, I remember telling him that I was leaving, as anything I might say that that point I would undoubtedly regret.

My first call on my way to the office was to Martin, who said he would back me, and then to another large investor, who said that he would back me as long as I reversed the trend of growing losses quickly. With my shares and the investors I called, I had the majority of the shareholders on my side. I went into the board meeting, guns blazing. Since I had poured my heart and soul into TerraCycle for almost a decade, and because I felt that my strategy was the right one (save for the lack of it making money) I cleaned house. Over the coming months we replaced half of the board of directors, along with a host of senior staff members. The line was effectively drawn between those who wanted TerraCycle to focus solely on worm poop and those who saw the value of sponsored waste and wanted us to be more.

After reflecting on the state of our financials throughout my time with TerraCycle, I have a confession to make: I am a chronic overprojector. This fact has even been reported on, on several occasions, by the *New York Times*. In May 2008 I was quoted predicting that our revenue would be "an estimated $8.5 million this year." We actually finished the year at $6.6 million. In June 2010, I thought we'd hit sales of "$16 million in 2010." We finished the year at $13.5 million.

A writer for *The New York Times Magazine*, Rob Walker, had this to say about TerraCycle in May 2007: "The privately held start-up can get a little carried away with its own hype at times. In 2005, the company projected sales of $3 million; it ended up selling a little less than $500,000. In 2006, the company said it expected annual sales of $2.5 million; the actual figure turned out to be a bit under $1.6 million." The writer went on to quote our head of public relations, Albe Zakes, as calling me "very optimistic"—but he also reported that "even the actual figures represent a solid growth record."

We have had strong growth, ranking as the 288th

fastest-growing private company in America in 2009, according to *Inc.* magazine (between 2009 and 2012 we made the list four times). Our sales have grown from $77,000 in 2004 to $500,000 in 2005 to $1.6 million in 2006 to $3.3 million in 2007 to $6.6 million in 2008 to $7.3 million in 2009, to $13.5 million in 2010, to $14.2 million in 2011, and so on.

So why do I keep overprojecting? I can assure you I'm not doing it maliciously or even consciously.

Investors—especially venture capital investors—demand aggressive "hockey stick" growth curves for revenue and profit. They want big multiples, and they want them in short time frames. If they don't see optimism, if they aren't buying into a dream, they are reluctant to invest. I can tell you first-hand that the flip side is the challenging conversations that inevitably follow—when you have to explain to your investors why you failed to live up to your projections. Fortunately, most of the investors I've worked with have been understanding and patient and have continued to believe in the vision that brought them to the company in the first place.

After the dust settled we still had to quickly solve the problems of profits and creating realistic expectations. As we had broadened what we manufactured, our margins decreased, often well into the negative. It had taken us four years to bottle worm waste profitably, and adding sewing lines and other manufacturing lines to our factory only compounded the margin issues. We hardly had any in-house experience with these new manufacturing supply chains, and the products we were making had put us into competition with very strong, typically China-based, manufacturing firms. As a result, we had to drop many of our prices below our costs, just to get the business.

We were also operating in multiple segments of the retail market. Our backpacks, pencil cases, and several other products sold in "Back to School," whereas seed starters and fertilizers were in "Home and Garden" and our wrapping paper and bows were sold in the "Holiday" segment. This required having a sales team that was versatile in multiple categories.

The issue was simple. We were a fertilizer company, and we knew nothing about making the kinds of products we were trying to make. We needed another business model.

Walking through a Walmart one day, I noticed that Disney and Nickelodeon seemed to have products in every category, from backpacks to stationery to shower curtains to food products. Obviously, there was no way these media companies could be expert in so many consumer product categories, so I investigated. A good friend and board member, Brett Johnson, helped me to understand the licensing model. Disney merely provided the characters and styles; other companies designed and manufactured the products and paid Disney a healthy licensing fee (typically 5–15 percent of net sales). I knew TerraCycle could fit the same model, with a small twist. We would collect the waste and design the products and processes but find best-in-class manufacturers and licensees to help us make, market, and sell the products and TerraCycle would help with the sales and marketing.

Under this new concept, TerraCycle would sell the raw materials (waste) to licensing companies—which themselves are manufacturers that use factories throughout the world. The licensees have large sales forces that deal regularly with all the big retailers so the products would be well represented in their respective markets. TerraCycle would earn income by charging a material sales fee and, in some cases, a licensing fee.

This change, which began in late 2008, led us to shut down all of TerraCycle's manufacturing. We moved from having 150 workers doing everything from bottling worm poop and sewing bags to just collecting the waste, converting it into raw materials (via third-party partners), and then selling the converted waste (as a new raw material) to manufacturing companies from Rubbermaid to Timberland. These companies would then make everything from trash cans to shoes from the waste.

Starting in 2009, even our worm poop fertilizer became a licensing deal. This, fittingly, was the last product to go. In perhaps a sentimental way we decided to keep the brewing of the worm poop in its original locale. Today, our headquarters in Trenton, which was entirely converted to office space after this transition, still brews worm poop.

The Art of Keeping One's Job

Under this new business model, TerraCycle grew to more than $13.5 million in sales in 2010; losses decreased from $4.5 million in 2008 to $1 million in 2010. The following year we grew sales to $14.2 million and for the first time in our history made a profit.

Right around the time of the infamous attempted coup I got a call from Brazil.

CHAPTER 14

The Micro-Multinational

The phone call came in 2008 from Pep-siCo (Frito-Lay) in Brazil. The company's executives liked how we were making chip bags nationally recyclable in the United States (by 2008 we were collecting more than 1 million chip bags per month in the United States), and they wanted to do the same thing in Brazil. As we've done with many brands, we had developed a national collection program for Frito's nonrecyclable waste—its chip bags. People all across America could now collect used bags and send them to TerraCycle. We cover the cost of shipping and pay two cents per chip bag to the charity or school of the collector's choice (all funded by Frito-Lay in efforts to make its nonrecyclable waste recyclable). We then take the bags and convert them into materials ranging from branded fabrics to plastic pellets. Our team then works with major manufacturing companies to use the new stuff in their products (through our newly formed licensing model), effectively replacing the need for virgin materials. As an example, Olivet, a major supplier to Walmart, now uses "chip-bag plastic" from TerraCycle as the plastic in the coolers it makes. This renders the chip bag nationally recyclable and produces a major win for the brands and their sustainability goals.

The executives with PepsiCo Brazil indicated that, if we weren't prepared to open operations in Brazil, they would pay us to teach a local company how to replicate our business. It immediately became clear to me that if we didn't seize the opportunity in other countries, someone else would get there first, and we'd never get another chance.

Thus began an aggressive multinational expansion. By 2012 we were operating in twenty-two countries from the United States to Turkey. That year we had just under $16 million in revenue and slightly more than one hundred employees, and we were operating all over the world—with local staff, operations, bank accounts, incorporations, and headaches. In 2012 about 35 percent of our annual revenue came from our operations outside the United States.

The Micro-Multinational

I think many small-business owners are reluctant to go global until they are fully established domestically. While such a strategy can seem logical, I would argue that going global is not as complicated as it used to be. Perhaps we are at the dawn of a new age of business, the age of the *micro-multinational*.

After learning through many mistakes with our first few countries, the trick to such rapid expansion, I believe, is having a replicable business model that can be executed with simplicity and good oversight.

Our business model is built on taking nonrecyclable waste items—such as pens and cigarette butts—and making them recyclable by creating national collection and solution systems. For us, it helps that most of our clients are already major multinationals (Kraft, GlaxoSmithKline) and that waste is a global issue with relatively few differences from one market to another regarding what is and isn't recyclable. Used pens, chewing gum, and cigarette butts are not recyclable anywhere in the world.

When we open an office in a new country, we do it with a simple formula. First we find a partner, which for us is usually a brand interested in running a collection program for its nonrecyclable waste. By policy, we will not open in a country before we have at least one partnership deal with a local company, and we prefer two. As a result, our out-of-pocket risk is limited to the travel and time we invest in finding those deals.

Once a deal is agreed upon, we look to hire a local leader. Initially we tried exporting our American staff to handle foreign deals, but this was a modest disaster. The problems—usually involving customer service or sales—stemmed from not understanding how things are done locally and not gaining that local trust.

I suspect that people put up their guard a little when doing business with a company where the staffers are all foreigners. A local leader is also better able to navigate local issues (from permits to hiring). Once a leader is hired we set up shop, which includes incorporating, opening bank accounts, finding office and warehouse space, and negotiating deals with all of our operational service providers, including logistics partners, lawyers, and accountants.

Once that is done, the local leader is charged with building the business while staying within the framework that has been developed by our global headquarters in Trenton. For example, we opened in the United Kingdom in September 2009 with one person. By 2012 that office had a staff of more than twenty.

As we grew internationally we faced a number of unique challenges. For example, employment taxes can make hiring the right person difficult. I love Brazil and its progressive

174

attitude toward sustainability, but it is frustrating to have to pay close to 100 percent taxes on every employee there. I also learned that it is critical to have local people doing local work. Public relations and customer service are great examples. To work effectively with media and customers, we need someone who knows not only the language but the local customs and norms. When we tried to manage our British public relations and customer service from the United States, we had no success. The moment we hired local representatives, our media interest and customer engagement took off.

While every country has a garbage problem, they have different business and garbage systems, along with different consumer attitudes, customs, retail demands, regulations, and everything else. After six months in Mexico, we had fantastic PR, but very few people had signed up for our program collecting Tang pouches. We realized that in some countries not as many consumers use the Internet for daily communications, so we had to rethink our outreach strategy. We began to focus on phone communications and leveraging local nonprofits to function as our ambassadors, and our collections quickly grew to record rates.

Managing a global company can be complex. By 2012, our Trenton, New Jersey, operation employed more than sixty-five people, but none of our foreign entities had more than twenty employees. When we begin operations in a new country, we hire a local general manager who works from his or her home; has no staff; and wears the PR, customer service, operations, business development, and client management hats all at once—just like a proper start-up. To maintain global oversight, our team leads in the United States are responsible for managing their counterparts in the rest of the world. Each country's local general manager reports to me and each of the United States team leads in their areas of responsibility.

As we grew I grappled with the question of transparency. Early on, I leaned toward limiting their information as I didn't want people worrying about something that wasn't their job and becoming distracted and unproductive. The problem was that when challenges came up I felt pretty much alone on them—and the staff was left guessing what was happening. Predictably, the lack of information fueled rumors and damaged morale.

Slowly, as I matured, my mind-set migrated to the other side of this question. Today, I'm inclined to give as much transparency as possible. I say "as much as possible" because we don't really give total transparency. Human resource matters (such as company payroll or stock options), legal matters (of all kinds), and certain financial matters (like merger deals we're working on) are not shared with the entire team.

But outside of these areas, our transparency is proactive and constant. All of our employees see everything—from what we invoiced that month to positive and negative changes with our clients—and they see it in great detail. In 2010 we started a biweekly reporting structure that requires every employee to send a report to his or her manager. The manager then comments back to the employee and then compiles the reports into a master departmental report.

Finally, this master report is then sent to every employee in the business every two weeks. One week we do our U.S. departments; the following week we do international. I review each report and write detailed feedback to each department—trying to be very frank—and that feedback is also sent to every employee. As a result, Mechi, for example, who manages public relations for TerraCycle Argentina, will receive the same reports as Michael, our global vice president of brigades.

The benefits of this method are astronomical. All of our employees know exactly what is going on and can learn from what other departments are doing. It creates a feeling of ownership and trust, and it has fostered communication. It also brings issues to the forefront much faster than ever before and serves as our critical feedback engine—the feedback given by myself and by managers is not just fluff. So employees always know how they are doing and how their performance compares to their peers.

We also started relying on incubators again, like in the EcoComplex back in the early worm poop days. Our first experience with an international incubator was in Brazil. This started by us selling a part of our Brazilian operation to a group called Warehouse Investimentos, which was led by a group of guys that wanted to bring the U.S. incubator model to Brazil. They invested, and we moved into a new funky office space and in the process saved about 50 percent on our cost of administrative services (human resources, legal, and accounting).

Similarly, we partnered with an incubator in Budapest called Colabs (ironic, as it sounds like "collapse" when you hear it) and located our Budapest TerraCycle team there.

In 2012 Jan Patrick, CEO of Landbell, our partner in Germany, called me, telling me about a big idea he was thinking of. Why not start a waste incubator in Berlin? After discussing it further we came to the idea of hosting a European competition where people from anywhere in the world could submit a waste-focused business concept, and we would judge them and invite the winner to join the incubator. TerraCycle would join by moving its German offices from Mainz to Berlin.

So perhaps incubators are great not only if you are a start-up with fewer than ten employees, but also if you are a micro-multinational with foreign offices with fewer than ten employees.

In four short years we moved from being a company that operated in North America only to operating in twenty-two countries—collecting garbage and processing it into new materials and products.

CHAPTER **15**

Negative Cost Marketing

Publicity has always been crucial to Ter-
raCycle's growth. And while what we've learned about how to
get publicity can be applied to any company, eco-capitalist or
not, there are some unique aspects to TerraCycle's publicity
strategy.

TerraCycle would not exist today without publicity. That
first summer, in 2002, Jon and I were just about ready to close
up shop and sell the worm gin, when Suman responded to the
interview we did on the radio. We were just about to run out
of money again, when we won the Carrot Capital business
plan contest—it wasn't Carrot's money that saved the day
(since we didn't get any), it was the huge amount of publicity

that came not only from winning, but from turning it down. Then, when the Scotts suit threatened to put us out of business, the publicity we generated with suedbyscotts.com was the biggest single factor (I think) in making the company come to terms with us in a way that gave us room to grow.

Naturally I'm not recommending to any small business that it turn down a heavyweight investor or try to be sued by its largest competitor just to get press. But I am recommending that whatever happens, try to find the right angle to turn it into good publicity.

As I said, TerraCycle had some unique aspects that attracted publicity right from the beginning. I would never discount the importance of the words "worm poop," for instance. If we had found a way to make organic waste from Princeton's dining halls into compost super quickly and super cheaply, it would have been a great piece of business, but most people in the media would have put it on the stack of worthy but not exciting start-ups. "Worm poop" made everybody take notice and remember.

Of course, you can't suddenly add something unexpected and surprising to your business just to attract attention, but you can make the most of your opportunities. If we had insisted that everyone say we were making "vermicompost tea," we would have been dead in the water. On a side note, it did take a lot of time and convincing to get our staff to stop saying "vermicompost" and start proclaiming "worm poop." The funny thing about the term "worm poop" is that it was more or less just a TerraCycle thing, and we could say it over and over again in interviews. Plus, it provides for great comic relief, and most journalists aren't expecting to laugh when getting pitched. Having a good worm poop joke or two makes our pitch fun and memorable, and that makes media more interested.

In the end everyone has a story—I think the magic is to find it and articulate it in a way that is compelling and approachable and makes one smile.

The trick to PR is offering an interesting and timely story. Luckily, TerraCycle's is both. Audiences loved the story of Marley's revival. When I dropped out of Princeton, that became part of the story, too—everyone loves hating the establishment, and dropping out of Princeton to sell worm poop takes the cake. You see the same story with Seth Goldman at Honest Tea and Gary Erickson at Clif Bar, both of whom left their careers and started other ones. What could be better than starting a business in your mother's kitchen and living the American dream? This is a story everyone can relate to. Our Sued by Scotts campaign provided a similar attraction—people love to root for the underdog, the dropout, the comeback kid.

So from the start, TerraCycle was more than just a product, it was an intriguing and inspiring story. This heartfelt human-interest backstory helped us get noticed by media big and small (plus a lot of hard work on our part, of course!). That's phase one of the art of publicity. Everyone always says that when you launch a company you'll get press, but once that initial burst subsides, you'll need to advertise, because marquee media like the *Wall Street Journal* won't keep writing about the same company again and again. While that's true to a certain extent, TerraCycle is living proof that there are ways to keep the media coming back for more. We have not once paid for an advertisement—and we won't—in 2007 and 2008 alone, the *Wall Street Journal* wrote nine articles either in the paper or on its Web site about TerraCycle.

In fact, we have seen an exponential growth in publicity since the beginning, growing from twenty-one articles in 2003 (around 2.5 million impressions) to more than five thousand articles in 2011 (more than 1 billion impressions).

And it's cheap. In 2007 we spent $100,000 on the entire publicity department (including salaries) and in 2012 we were spending about $500,000 per year globally—that's about $100 per article. How does a business continue to generate publicity when it is no longer the new kid on the block? What are the golden rules of attaining a growing volume of PR? And most important, how do you get the same places to keep writing about you? Here's what I've learned.

Do not hire a public relations firm. This is the most important rule, in my opinion, for one simple reason: if PR firms were really in the business of getting you press, they should be paid only for every article produced about a given client. The formula would be something like: the amount of space/time given to the story multiplied by the value of that space. In other words, the PR firm would earn more the longer a magazine or a television show spends on a client or if the article gets syndicated. A brief mention in a blog would means the firm would earn less. With this utopian viewpoint, I have yet to find a PR firm that will accept.

Also, journalists—according to my friends who are journalists—strongly prefer to talk with the business owners or someone from the company instead of with an outside consultant. Journalists are always looking for an angle that no one else has found or an angle that will appeal strongly to their particular audience. Naturally, they feel they are going to get that from the company rather than from an intermediary. That leads to my next rule.

If you are going to do it yourself, remember a press release is the story. Many journalists are overworked, and if you can give them a prepackaged story, you're golden. Most press releases are boring and long and don't really tell a story. A product announcement, for instance, is not a story—but it could be. It is important to remember that the story is in the eye of the beholder. I'm sure that you have had a grandpa at some point go on and on (passionately, mind you) about some mundane event. Well, that's a story because your grandpa chose it to be. A killer press release is one that the publishers can print word for word if they choose to. Oh yeah, and it's all about the headline! The headline will make or break your release.

At TerraCycle, Albe has made it a rule to tailor every press release to the place it's going to. Instead of looking like a piece of boilerplate that was defrosted from the back of the freezer, it reads like a letter, beginning with a recognition of the needs, interests, and audience of the magazine or newspaper. If a release about TerraCycle Plant Food is going to the AARP magazine editor, it will talk about how senior citizens need to take special care about what chemicals are going into the house— for themselves, their pets, and their children and grandchildren. If a release is going to the *New Yorker*, it will talk about how green is the new black, how the plant food is easy to use and so environmentally friendly that it will make the reader feel instantly cool.

Journalists hate to get generic, canned releases. At TerraCycle, we have mastered the art of the quick study. Take a few moments to make sure you have the right editor at the right publication and that you have a pitch perfectly oriented for their coverage area and audience. A lot of publicity departments will do that for the major media—at least they will do it in person—but TerraCycle applies the principle to everybody, small or large. As we've seen, local newspapers have been a terrific boost to TerraCycle. Which brings me to the next rule.

Negative Cost Marketing

———

Focus on local papers. Did you know that there are more than ten thousand local papers across America? And each is produced by a tiny number of people! They don't have enough people to cover the local baseball game or the school bake sale, so they often cannot get enough local content to fill up their pages. Our brigades, or collection points, are all local stories. When a location (like a school) signs up or hits a collection milestone, we provide the newspaper not just with a description of the program and the good it does but also with pictures of schoolchildren and teachers and quotes from them about what a great thing TerraCycle is doing for the environment and the organization. It's exactly the kind of story a local newspaper values. Sure, a *Wall Street Journal* article is better for attracting investors or new clients. But most average Americans get their news from their local paper, not from national publications. So no matter if the paper has a circulation of 5,000 or 500,000, in that geographic area that paper is *the* most trusted, and often most overlooked, news source.

In the end, though, PR, like any form of convincing, is a result of hard work. That means working the phones, not the wire. Most people, once they've written their press release, feed it into the newswire and think their job is done because their story is so good. But if you really want publicity, you can't stop there. You need to call, e-mail, and keep calling. Call to make sure the press release arrived, call to see if there's anything that they need, and then call with another reason why the product is perfect for their readers. Editors and writers get hundreds of e-mails a day; they may not read your press release.

So you have to call and call until you get them on the phone. Once you're on the phone, you have to care about the story and be passionate about it in order to make them care. Also, research the writer before you call. If you're asking writers to invest time in a story about your idea, you have to invest a little in them. Make friends with the writers—if you have a good product and give them the right information, you are doing them a favor and they will remember it. Plus, always be respectful of their time and their ever-looming deadlines. Journalists have editors and publishers to make happy and deadlines to hit on a daily basis, so be aware of the constraints on their time. Always start your call by asking if they have a moment to hear a story that is perfectly suited for their "beat." If they say no, ask to schedule a better time to talk. Journalists will appreciate your awareness and consideration. If they are available to talk, then get right to the point. Journalists want a pitch that is concise and easy to understand; giving them too much information at once will only distract them and confuse your message.

Also, help journalists do their job—after all, they are doing you a big favor by covering you. Journalists are like most folks—they have a job, and their job is to write relevant, timely, and fun articles and to make sure that those articles sell more newspapers and magazines. To do this they may need to interview lots of people around the story (which takes their time), do some research (which takes more time), and send a photographer to take some pictures (which takes more time and money). To get journalists excited to write about you, try to help them do their job. Before you send out your press release, have quotes already prepared and interviews lined up for them; have background research on the topic, and independent analysts or experts familiar with your company and your industry, available for them; and always have high-resolution, well-shot photographs ready to go. By making the journalist's job easier, the likelihood of an article will go up and the chances of getting a longer, more robust article will skyrocket. This will make journalists respect and want to work with you in the future. If they know you can supply everything they need for a solid article, they will take the time to listen to a future pitch.

For example, when we launched a display in OfficeMax we were able to achieve more than sixty articles on that one display program; when we launched our cigarette waste collection program in Canada we had three hundred articles in one month.

Publicity is especially important for small companies. Ironically, big companies typically see publicity as a risk. They would prefer to control the message, which is something they can do with advertising. Publicity, which is almost by definition written by someone outside the company, becomes more a matter of risk management than positive attention for them. If you're a small, growing business, do not fall into that trap. Publicity is the greatest asset you have—just because you are small and growing. America is built on the dream of starting your own business, the rags-to-riches story even when you don't have the riches yet. The media will treat you as their hero if you can demonstrate how you are fulfilling that dream. Dan Rather and CBS were willing to give us five minutes on the national evening news even when we barely had any customers. Whether you're being sued or starting a new business, publicity can be your biggest tool.

So if phase one is to get lots of PR, then phase two is to become the media, unlocking the potential of negative cost media. In 2011 we generated over $200,000 of revenue from negative cost media. This is the key turning point, when you go from just being written about frequently to doing the writing yourself.

The number of media outlets has grown dramatically over the past one hundred years, not just in form but also in variety. The number of radio stations has grown in parallel with the emergence of TV, cable television, the Internet, and so on. Consequently, there is a dramatic need for content and there is not enough available.

Moreover, as people have grown up with a medium, they have taken greater and greater control of it. Once a generation had grown up on national network television, there was a drive for more individual, more local, and more topic-specific kinds of programs. Cable television filled that need, and people began making their own television programs. The invention of the handheld video camera made it possible for almost anyone to produce a television show. The number of talk shows, reality shows, and call-in shows increased dramatically.

The Internet brought this spread of media and of individually produced media to its zenith. There is a big opportunity to start creating your content. This can be as simple as starting to write your own blog—most businesses have their own blogs these days. Once you become the creator of the content, you can become the expert and be invited onto shows for your expertise in the subject. For example, Wendy Bounds, a reporter who was our first contact with the *Wall Street*

Journal, now has a weekly show on CNBC to discuss her specialty, small business.

The big realization came to me after the editors from *Inc.* magazine, which had written seven articles about TerraCycle, contacted me about writing a blog for them. I had written a piece about the Scotts suit for their Web site, and at the beginning of 2008 they were starting several new blogs. They asked if I would write about eco-capitalism. I began with a post called "The Secret Formula for Generating Crazy Amounts of PR." Don't worry about looking it up; you're reading it—it's the basis for this chapter.

From there I started getting more blogs, from *Packaging Digest* to *Treehugger.com* to the *New York Times* (which happens to pay a modest stipend). Blogs that pay you are a clear and achievable example of negative cost media.

By getting lots of media coverage and by writing blogs you become an expert. And being an expert gets you invited to give speeches at universities and conferences. For me this started happening about three years after starting TerraCycle, and by 2012 I had an official speaking agent and was making a respectable salary on the side by giving talks. Many on our team, from Albe to Michael, give talks regularly, getting themselves flown around the world and sometimes even paid to spread the message about TerraCycle.

After speeches can come writing books. Think about this very book you are reading. By now you are an expert in Terra-

Cycle and hopefully you like what we're all about. The publication of the book itself creates more publicity, and that publicity will generate more brigades, more sales, more awareness, which in turn will generate more publicity.

The idea of generating books even moved to our waste design department, which puts out a design book about how you can create products from waste at home every once in a while. We are even working on a graffiti coffee table book as a documentation of the incredible amount of art that has been painted on the TerraCycle office walls.

A yearly design book is sort of like a magazine that puts out one nice issue every year. So moving to a magazine is not a far stretch. Brands such as Martha Stewart and Rachael Ray all have a host of media assets from magazines to books to even TV shows.

Our quest for a TV show started in 2008 when I realized that we were having various news cameras coming through the office on a weekly basis. In other words, what we had was good TV.

In the world of TV you typically start with a TV agent. Luckily my book agent, Alan, worked at the time at a company called the Firm. The Firm represented everyone from Leonardo DiCaprio to Cameron Diaz. I once rode up the elevator with Cameron and her then boyfriend, Criss Angel. Paul, the lead TV agent at the Firm, took us under his wing. We met first with a number of production companies, and after finding one that was a good fit, we produced a demo. (As a side note, try to get the production company to produce to demo on its own nickel.) We then took the demo to a few dozen networks, where we pitched a docudrama around TerraCycle. Every episode would follow a different waste stream from being a problem to us finding and launching an actual solution to it. After running around Los Angeles and New York we accumulated an overwhelming number of rejections and paused our pursuits for a while.

A few months later, I met a production company that was filming at our offices for a piece for the Discovery Channel. We chatted, and things clicked, and a few months later our child, *Garbage Moguls*, the first TerraCycle TV show, was born, on the National Geographic Channel.

All of these models, from a TV show to a book to blogging, are forms of negative cost media. You get paid for creating content about yourself. It's credible and profitable.

CHAPTER 16

The Nasties

In 2009 we were approached by Noma-
corc, the leaders in the production of synthetic wine corks, to
run a cork brigade. At the time we needed millions of corks to
create a corkboard product that OfficeMax was ordering
from us, and we concluded that wine, as controlled vices go,
is rather innocuous. In the end, there wasn't much internal
debate, so we partnered rather quickly with the alcohol industry.

I preface this chapter by saying that by 2009 we had been
approached by all three "merchant of death" industries that
are highlighted in the movie *Thank You for Smoking*. All three

industries have waste streams that are not recyclable. Among others: alcohol has wine corks, guns have shotgun shells, and tobacco has cigarette butts. For us, the question boils down to this: Should we censor the products we collect and recycle? Or should we collect any product that advances TerraCycle's mission of eliminating waste?

In the case of wine corks, bullet casings, and cigarette butts, the intention is consistent with TerraCycle's core mission: to find recycling and/or upcycling solutions for waste. There may be a legitimate debate as to whether certain industries should exist, but so long as they do exist, shouldn't we try to minimize their waste? I've had long arguments with friends in the natural products industry who claim that by collecting the waste of nonorganic products, TerraCycle is validating companies whose products are "less good." I argue that TerraCycle's job is to collect and repurpose the vast amounts of waste generated by all companies and their consumers—not to judge whether one company or product is better than another. If we apply this logic to alcohol, guns, and tobacco, I think the answer is clear: we should accept the waste of legal products and let the law and the market work out which products thrive and fail.

To that effect, in 2012 we launched partnerships in both Canada and the United States with Big Tobacco, perhaps the most prolific and infamous "merchant of death."

Regardless of what we think of tobacco, we can all agree

that the litter caused by cigarette butts is a major issue. In Texas, the Department of Transportation has estimated that more than 130 million cigarette butts will find their way onto Texas highways this year. Globally, it has been estimated that more than a trillion butts make their way into our environment as discarded waste every year.

Our solution involves separating the paper, tobacco, and ash from the filter. The organic materials are then composted properly, leaving the part that looks like white cotton but is actually a form of plastic called cellulose acetate (while this material can be made from organic materials, almost all cigarette makers use plastics). The cellulose acetate is then sanitized and injection-molded into a plastic that can be used for a variety of uses, such as plastic pallets and car berms for factories.

Our intention was to require as little change as possible in the habits of today's smokers. That means that if you are at a bar or your home you keep using your regular ashtrays. The only change is that you empty the trays into any plastic bag and place that bag in a box (like a shoebox or whatever you may have lying around). When the box is full, you download a free shipping label from our Web site and send it to Terra-Cycle to be recycled. We offer a $1 donation to your favorite charity for every pound of butts collected.

We also launched a pocket version, the Butt Sack; it's a small envelope (with aluminum inside for fire safety) with a preprinted mailing label on it. You put your smoked butts in it on the go. When it's full, you simply drop it in the mail.

I was a little nervous when, in 2012, we launched the world's first national program for cigarette waste in Canada. Surprisingly the media didn't grill us for partnering with Big Tobacco. Instead they applauded us, with three hundred positive articles in the first thirty days alone. Soon, tobacco companies called from all over the world asking for a similar solution in their local markets.

In 2012 we also developed the first solution to recycle dirty diapers. The process allows for collection primarily from nurseries (for baby diapers) and at hospitals and elderly care facilities (for adult diapers). The collected diapers are then irradiated to kill the pathogens and shredded and separated. The resulting material can then be recycled into new materials and later new products.

2012 also marked the launch of the world's first national program to collect used chewing gum (in Brazil). The gum is collected in special balls that attach to fences and the full balls are mailed to TerraCycle, where we have them melted into a plastic.

What I realized by taking on the harder waste streams, from cigarette butts to used tampons, is that there is really no such thing as waste. All waste can be either reused, upcycled, or recycled into something new. So far with no clear exception.

CHAPTER 17

Conclusion: Eliminating the Idea of Waste

Waste doesn't exist in nature. If you could talk to a tree and you said, "Hey, Mr. Tree, could you tell me what garbage is?" the tree couldn't reply to you, as the word "garbage" or "waste" doesn't exist in nature. The output of every system is the most important input of the next system. The leaf that falls off a tree is very important for the bugs that eat it and the plants that later grow from it. We breathe the oxygen that a tree releases as a by-product, just as a tree needs to breathe our by-product, carbon dioxide.

Waste is entirely a man-made concept. And moreover it is a very modern idea. Before the Second World War people made things from simple materials—wood, cotton, and other things that nature knew what to do with. And people didn't consume the way we do today. A table in the past was made from wood and made to last. It would pass down between generations, avoiding the need for new tables, and if at some point it broke, it would be fixed. When, no longer repairable, it finally hit the end of its life, it would compost and become food for the millions of microbes that ate it, converting it into soil.

After the war, the world found itself traumatized and in need of a major economic recovery. Also around the same time, we saw the emergence of mass-produced, affordable, complex materials, such as plastics. The solution to our desires for economic prosperity and a new, higher standard of living became mass-produced disposable products. We could now make things cheaply and in great quantities, allowing mankind to enter into the age of consumption. And since then our rate of waste creation per person has exploded. By 2005 each American discarded 4.6 pounds of waste per day, double what it was in 1960, which itself was even more than what we threw out prior to 1940. All this was driven by our growing appetite to buy stuff, and that stuff being made from complex materials and having a disposable nature.

Today that same table isn't made from high-quality, simple materials (like oak) and passed down from generation to generation. Instead we drive to Ikea and buy a table that will barely last a few years, let alone generations. Then when its useful life is finished, since it's made from plastic or another composite, it doesn't easily degrade and we throw it in a pile we call a landfill.

Waste also defies the standard parameters of typical supply-and-demand economics. Go to Google and search for images of "supply-demand curve" and you will find hundreds of examples of "price" (beginning at zero) on the vertical axis and "quantity" (also beginning at zero) on the horizontal axis. Basically, the curves show that prices increase as supply goes down, and the converse, but I have yet to find a "supply-demand" curve that focuses on what happens in the negative—in other words, the concept of "negative demand," taking into account the price someone would pay to dispose of an item.

Waste is simply any commodity that we are willing to pay to get rid of. It is the only commodity in the world that has true negative value. Waste exists partly because of economics, because in many cases it is cheaper to throw out something than to reuse it or properly recycle it, and companies have yet to be required to maintain responsibility for the entire life cycle of their products.

This is where TerraCycle comes in. We believe that by creating national collection and solution programs for waste we can help people and companies solve the problem of waste.

By 2012, many major global corporations in more than twenty-two countries had voluntarily contracted for sponsored waste programs with TerraCycle, taking responsibility for their waste in cooperation with their consumers who collect it. In 2012 we also launched the first version of our program where consumers can do the same. They can pay for the solution to their nonrecyclable waste, if a brand hasn't decided to pay for that category of waste yet.

If we can create programs that produce demand for waste, and if people participate in them, then as collection volumes rise, more and more of our waste will have a positive value. It will simply stop becoming waste.

With all this said, the true solution to waste isn't TerraCycle. Think about it. Everything becomes waste sometime, and living things produce waste during their productive lives. In our human systems, we need to return to treating waste the way nature does—by utilizing its value. In this context, TerraCycle is just another way that nature is organizing and reorganizing, helping humans restore a more natural balance to how we produce and consume. Using less is the best approach, and when you are purchasing something, buy something that will last and give others joy when you are done with it.

So now that you've completed reading this book, consider giving it to a friend.